NORFOLK COLLEGE LIBRARY

D1632585

JOHN HEDGECOE'S
COMPLETE GUIDE TO
Black and White
Photography

THE COLLEGE OF WEST ANGLIA

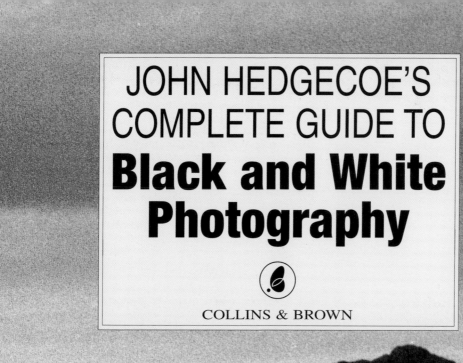

JOHN HEDGECOE'S
COMPLETE GUIDE TO
Black and White
Photography

COLLINS & BROWN

First published in Great Britain in 1994
Revised and updated in 2005
by Collins & Brown
The Chrysalis Building
Bramley Road
London W10 6SP

An imprint of **Chrysalis** Books Group plc

Copyright © Collins & Brown Limited 2005

Text copyright © Collins & Brown and John Hedgecoe 2005

Illustrations copyright © John Hedgecoe 2005

The right of John Hedgecoe to be identified as the author of this work has been
asserted by him in accordance with the Copyright, Designs and Patents Act, 1988.

All rights reserved. No part of this publication may be reproduced, stored in a
retrieval system, or transmitted in any form or by any means, electronic,
mechanical, photocopying, recording or otherwise, without the prior written
permission of the copyright owner.

1 3 5 7 9 8 6 4 2

British Library Cataloguing-in-Publication Data:
A catalogue record for this book
is available from the British Library.

ISBN 1 84340 316 1

770·28 HED

Conceived by Collins & Brown
ASSOCIATE WRITER: Chris George
DESIGNED BY: Rod Teasdale & Phil Kay

Reproduction by Typongraph, Italy
Printed and bound by Kyodo, Singapore

Contents

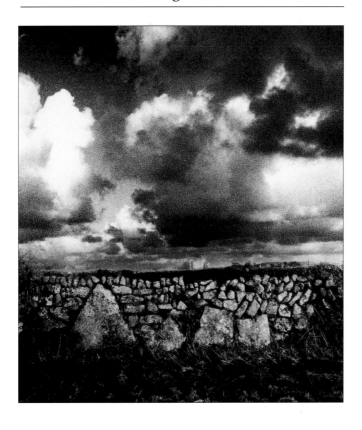

Introduction

DESPITE THE FACT that practically every image that is taken nowadays is in full colour, black and white still has a special attraction for serious photographers. Monochrome photographs are widely used on the advertising pages of glossy magazines and frequently found on the walls of exhibition halls. Furthermore, digital cameras and computer software has made it much easier for anyone to produce black and white images than ever before. But why does this seemingly old-fashioned medium have such an enduring appeal to professional and hobby photographers alike?

Learning about photography

For those interested in learning about photography as a means of self-expression, interpretation or as a creative outlet, then the black and white medium has much to offer. This is not to say that precisely the same learning process is not possible with colour photography; indeed many artistic images are successfully shot in colour. However, by removing colour from the subject you immediately take your photographs one step back from the depiction of a simple likeness. These monochrome images are at once divorced from the reality of the way we all see the world around us.

All photographs are an abstraction in one way or another. Even if the picture reveals a completely realistic and recognizable subject, it is only a two-dimensional representation of a three-dimensional scene – whether it is printed on paper, or displayed on a screen. Taking away the colour as well as the dimension of depth furthers this process of abstraction, and thus encourages you to make something of that scene that is truly unique, something that has to do only with the way that

▲ **Spatial ambiguity**

The simplification of this portrait of the English artist David Hockney to shades of grey has produced a type of ambiguity in which the artist seems to be on much the same plane as, and therefore a part of, the painting acting as a backdrop. The same shot would have far less impact in full colour.

▶ Morning light
Once colour is extracted, pictures of plants become studies in texture, form and shape. In order to capture the night's frost still fringing the leaves of these garden plants, it was necessary to shoot well before the sun reached them. By taking an exposure reading from the brightest highlight in the scene, the shadowy parts behind the foliage have been thrown into deep shadow, creating a strongly three-dimensional effect.

you see and interpret the subject in the camera's viewfinder. In other words, it allows you to stamp your own identity on the image.

Preconceived ideas

There are many preconceptions regarding the types of subject suitable for black and white and those that are best tackled in colour. Many people may feel, for example, that the black and white medium is most suitable for 'arty' pictures, those that are not concerned with normal, everyday 'humdrum' subject matter. Others say that portraits of men look fine in black and white because it can emphasize their masculinity while those of women really need the extra femininity that colour brings. Yet others say that photographs of nature or natural history subjects – such as landscapes, flowers, trees, and so on – seem flat and lifeless without colour, or question the point of taking location and holiday shots in black and white because you can't see what the place really looks like. None of this is in fact true.

There is no type of subject that is best shot in colour, nor any other that suits black and white better. The success of any photograph, taken on any type of film or with any type of digital camera, depends on the photographer's aesthetic sensitivity to capture the nature of the subject – on his or her perception, vision and imagination. Also vital is the technical ability to select the best aperture and shutter speed, the most appropriate viewpoint, focal length and the moment to shoot.

Although colour photography has been easily accessible to all for half a century, some of the most evocative and powerful images of recent years have been printed in black and white. Perhaps this is in part due to the fact that a black and white image allows the picture's audience to exercise its imagination – because the image is not in any way a literal rendition, there is no one way to interpret it. Another part of the answer may be that the black and white medium simplifies the image, stripping it down to its essential elements – light and shade, shape, form

◄ Window light

Positioning your subject adjacent to a window to take advantage of natural sunlight often produces a dramatically contrasty image, with some parts of the subject brightly lit while others are seen in deep shadow. And because all of the light is coming from just one direction – the window – texture is likely to be an important aspect of the composition, especially since there is no colour to compete for attention and distract the eye.

and texture – and, as a result, it can have much more of an impact.

The intention behind every photograph is to convey an idea. If you have a clearly thought-out notion of what that idea is then there is no reason why a black and white photograph of, say, a flower specimen – which, in reality, is bursting with vibrant colour – should not make a successful black and white study.

Taking control

One traditional advantage that black and white has over colour photography is that it is relatively simple to maintain control over the appearance of the final image, right through from taking the picture to developing the film and then finally printing up the resulting negatives. The really special thing about the black and white darkroom

is that processing still takes place in open trays. Even on your first attempt at processing and printing you should be able to achieve a reasonable image. And the magic of seeing your print start to appear in the developing tray after a few seconds never completely wears off.

The chemicals used in black and white film and paper developing are relatively inexpensive to buy when compared with their colour equivalents, and fewer of them are required. Black and white films and papers are also much more forgiving of any small processing errors you may make. The recommended temperature range for the critical stages of colour processing is harder to maintain accurately. Black and white processing and printing still needs some scientific vigour if you want consistent results. But the procedures are easier to get to grips with – allowing you to concentrate on aesthetic considerations.

Today, the digital darkroom allows you to exercise all the old tricks – and many new ones – using a standard desktop computer. Manipulation software allows you to refine and manipulate black and white images as simply as colour ones. Furthermore, these programs allow you to transform colour images into monochrome ones with incredible ease – and allow you to tint and tone black and white originals at speed.

It is by manipulating the tonal range – the shades of grey between black and white – that you control the mood and atmosphere of the monochrome image. The digital darkroom allows you much more precise control over this procedure than was ever possible using chemical baths and an enlarger. You can see the effect that a technique has immediately on screen without having to wait minutes for the print to develop – and if you make a wrong move you can go back one or more steps, without having to start again.

Light sources

An immensely liberating aspect of working in black and white is that you do not have to worry about the different colour temperatures of the various light sources you could use to illuminate your subjects.

All light has a specific colour temperature. Light from the sun or from a desk lamp looks

▼ Range of tones

By filling the foreground with haphazard and jagged shapes, all picked out in well-defined tones, the seedy and slightly derelict nature of this waterfront scene has been superbly conveyed.

pretty much the same colour to the human eye. This is mainly due to the fact that the brain adjusts our perception so that an object of a known colour – a white handkerchief, for example, or a green apple – illuminated by any regular type of light source appears to be the colour we know it should be.

However, colour film can make no such adjustment, and so colour photographers have to ensure that light sources with radically different colour temperatures are not used in the same shot. Digital cameras can correct for these colour differences automatically – but they do not always give perfect results, particularly when there are two or more light sources. When working in black and white, though, you can mix light from the sun with that from, say, ordinary domestic room lights with impunity, since the differences in colour will not show – although contrast may not then be consistent. Your concern is primarily the relative strengths of highlights and shadows and the overall intensity of the lighting available.

Filters

An obvious assumption to make is that a black and white image is not affected by the different colours in the world around us, but his is of course not the case. Instead of reproducing the different wavelengths of 'white' light as different colours, it reproduces them as different shades of grey.

▼ Double exposure

This intriguing night-time image was taken by first exposing the flame and tower through a tube of cardboard, and then covering the tube to shield that part of the film and moving the camera while the shutter remained open in order to cause the lights of the oil refinery to blur and streak.

▶ Ordering your priorities
The right framing and exposure, and selecting the best moment to shoot, are all far more important factors than whether or not the image is in colour or black and white. This portrait is so engaging that the absence of colour simply has no significance.

Black and white film basically reproduces dark colours as dark tones and light colours as light tones. However, it is not uniformly sensitive to all the different colours of light and this fact can lead to the tonal equivalents of some colours looking very similar when shot on black and white film.

The colour blue is an obvious example to use to illustrate this point, since it tends to print as a very pale tone. This can be a problem in landscape shots, for example, or in any picture in which an area of blue sky is prominent, since it will often appear as a featureless expanse of white – almost indistinguishable from any clouds that may also be present. You can burn in this part of the image by giving it extra exposure at the printing stage, or by using an appropriate Photoshop manipulation tool, but this can produce a grainy and unnatural-looking area of tone.

To overcome this type of problem, as well as to manipulate the tonal response of the film to convey a particular mood or atmosphere, you can use a wide range of coloured filters over the camera lens. An orange filter, for example, strengthens the film's tonal response to blue, thus making skies more prominent. A deep red filter has an even greater effect, turning a blue sky nearly black if the film is slightly underexposed as well. An orange filter can also be used to make vegetation appear as a darker tone; for the reverse effect use a green-coloured filter. These filters, however, are not usually used with digital cameras – as it is easier to shoot the image in colour and then apply the filter effects using image manipulation software.

How this book is organized
The first chapter is an introduction to the components that make up a successful black and white image, including the principles of basic composition and framing. In the next three chapters, dealing with the popular subject areas of still lifes, portraits and landscapes, you will see how these principles can be applied in many different areas of photography. The final two chapters of the book form a complete beginner's guide to both the digital and traditional darkroom – explaining the equipment and techniques needed to convert what the camera shoots into a perfectly polished black and white image.

Basic principles

L IKE ANY OTHER AREA of creative endeavour, good photography depends on the imagination, talent and application you are able to invest in the subject. There are, of course, certain constraints you need to recognize in order to achieve, for example, a 'properly' exposed image – one that contains the right distribution and densities of tones – from which to make a print. It is also important to understand the relationship between the lens aperture and camera shutter speed in terms of correct exposure and subject appearance. All modern cameras have some form of automatic exposure system. You may, however, want to override this in order to increase or decrease the area of sharp focus surrounding your subject (the 'depth of field'), by choosing a particularly small or wide aperture. Or you may want to take control of the settings in order to select a very brief or very long shutter speed – to freeze subject movement or to record it in a blurry, impressionistic fashion.

These technical aspects of photography can be quickly learned. What is harder, and takes much more time, though, is learning to translate in your mind's eye the colourful world you see around you into the range of black through white tones that your film will produce. This takes practice.

In the same way, there is no substitute for understanding how the angle of light, or competing light sources, influence the apparent shape or surface characteristics of your subject. Furthermore, it is important to understand how framing, camera angle and focal length all come together to create effective compositions.

▶ **Improvisation**
Interiors can often be difficult to shoot successfully in colour because of the mixture of different light sources. Working in black and white avoids this problem entirely. This softly lit scene allows the composition to concentrate on the amusing juxtaposition of a giant classical sculpture and the curator with his feather duster.

Colour into black and white

I T TAKES SOME practice to learn to see the world of colour in tones of grey. If you have access to two film cameras, one of the best ways to make this learning transition is to load one with colour slide film and the other with black and white film (print or slide). On a day with a good range of weather conditions – from clear skies with bright sun through to cloud and a more gloomy aspect – take a range of shots of the same subjects using both cameras.

Film types

For this learning exercise it is best to use colour slide film rather than colour negative film. Slide film gives extremely accurate colour rendition because it is designed to give a direct positive image without any intervening printing stage. It is rare to find a film laboratory, especially one using automatic processing machinery, that is capable of producing colour prints that are true to life across the whole range of colours.

Subject types

When choosing subjects for this exercise, look for variety. A broad view with plenty of foliage and a large expanse of blue sky with prominent clouds is a good example. This will allow you to see how the black and white film handles the different shades of green and, especially, the sky area: unless you use coloured filters over the lens, blue skies can often be disappointing in black and white (*see pp. 38–9*).

Try for close-up comparative shots as well. A boldly patterned multicoloured subject would be ideal to allow you to see how individual colours translate into black and white and also to see if the various shades of grey allow you to distinguish

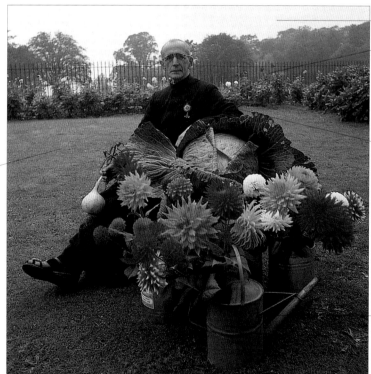

This reproduction shows an accurate balance of colours, as would be seen by the unaided eye.

Pale blue sky.

The railings and background foliage appear well separated.

The large expanse of green lawn seems to engulf the subject. Note how the colour is more saturated in the shadow areas.

The colour of the cassock is dominant here. There is no sense of how the material might feel if it was actually touched.

The watering cans are quite pronounced in colour.

The foreground flowers in reds, oranges and yellows contrast so powerfully with the surrounding green that they initially hold the viewer's attention away from the remainder of the composition.

between various colours when they are adjacent to each other.

Processing and printing

Whereas most people send colour films to a laboratory for processing, in black and white it is possible to handle this aspect at home in your own darkroom (*see pp. 116–21*). You will then have the chance to experiment with a variety of film and paper developers, each of which will produce slightly different tonal responses. The paper's contrast grade also has an effect on the appearance of the print (*see pp. 126–7*), as do such techniques as dodging and burning-in (*see p. 130*).

This reproduction shows the scene as it would appear if it were shot on black and white film with a pale orange filter over the lens.

The orange filter has produced a little tone in the sky, which otherwise would have appeared completely bleached out.

Background foliage and railings have reproduced as tonally very similar and don't show the same separation as in the colour version.

With colour removed, the cassock now has more of a tactile quality.

The orange filter has lightened the tonal reproduction of the flowers, which otherwise might have appeared too similar to the green of the cabbage.

Note how darker colours generally reproduce as darker tones, as compared with the lighter colours.

In black and white, the watering cans seem less pronounced.

Using a digital camera

B LACK AND WHITE PICTURES are easy to take with a digital camera. Most models provide a shooting mode or 'special effect' that will record the image in monochrome – usually found in one of the on-screen menu options. Often there will also be a sepia-toned shooting option, to give a warm-brown colour to your monochrome image

These options give you the advantage of being able to take a black and white shot, and revert back to shooting colour, whenever you want. There is no need to rewind and replace the film to do this. Furthermore, the LCD screen allows you to preview the shots in monochrome – removing the difficulty that film photographers face in visualizing how a world of colour will translate into shades of grey.

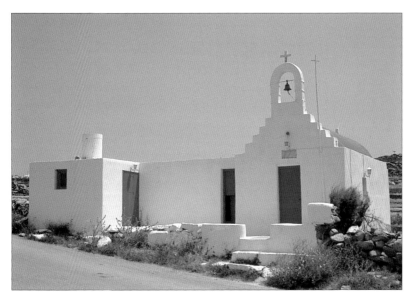

▲ B&W mode
Many digital cameras have a special effect mode that allows you to shoot images in black and white. This can provide a useful preview of what a scene will look like devoid of colour.

◄ Colour original
It is best practice to shoot scenes in colour even if you intend the final image to be displayed on screen or printed in monochrome.

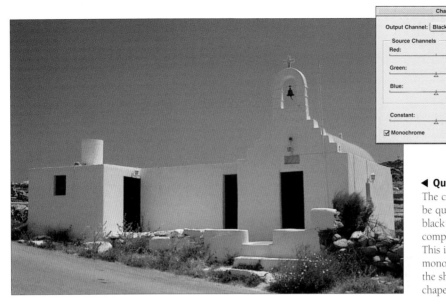

◀ Quick conversion
The colour images can be quickly converted to black and white on the computer in Photoshop. This is a straightforward monochrome version of the shot of the white chapel.

Many black and white digital photographers, however, actually shoot their monochrome pictures in full colour. The shot can easily be converted to black and white using a one-click operation with many image editing computer programs.

There is a twofold advantage to this approach. By retaining a colour file, you always have the option of using the shot in colour (not an option if you use a black and white shooting mode). More importantly for the serious monochrome worker, the conversion from colour becomes part of the creative process. You effectively get the chance to control the shade of grey that each particular hue within the scene becomes (see page 146). The blue of the sky in a landscape, for instance, can be made to appear darker, whilst the grass can be made into a lighter tone than a straight conversion would have provided. It is the digital equivalent of using coloured filters to affect tonal range, but you get much more control, and can experiment with different settings in the comfort of your own home.

Channels have been adjusted to make the sky a darker grey.

The walls of the building are now a slightly darker shade of grey.

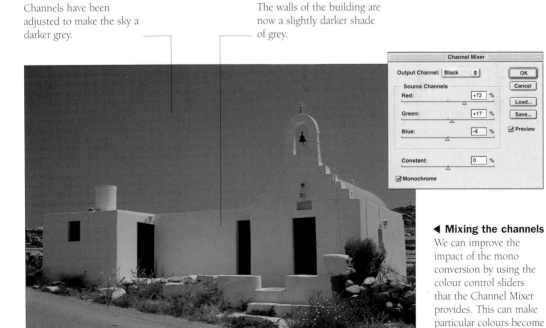

◀ Mixing the channels
We can improve the impact of the mono conversion by using the colour control sliders that the Channel Mixer provides. This can make particular colours become a darker or lighter grey.

Tonal range

INSTEAD OF COLOURS, a black and white image is composed of shades of grey – ranging between solid black and stark white. Unless your intention is to go for a high- or low-key image (*see pp. 22–3*), then the 'ideal' negative is one that you can print on a normal grade of paper – say, grade 2 (*see pp. 126–7*) – and that contains the widest possible range of grey tones between the two extremes. For a digital file this means the histogram for the image has values at all 256 levels of grey – with no gaps in the graph.

However, it is not unusual for photographers to expose a negative or digital image knowing that it will contain a restricted tonal range, and then to enhance this even further, either through their choice of developer and paper grade, or by Levels or Curves adjustment in the digital darkroom (*see pp. 150–1*) in order to suit the needs of the subject.

▲ Full tonal range

A complex scene, showing a range of patterns and textures, is ideal for making the most of the range of tones that black and white film is capable of reproducing. Here a lavish interior shows full complement of greys – from the whites in the bright windows, to the blacks in the unlit shadows.

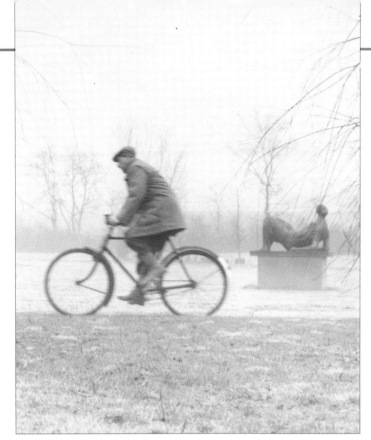

◀ Light-toned result

This portrait of the artist Henry Moore cycling past one of his sculptures has a tonal range restricted to the light end of the scale. The dark frame of his bicycle, the shadow area beneath his coat and the sculpture itself, however, help to, 'sharpen' the overall appearance of the print.

▼ Dark-toned result

This view of a refinery was taken against the light and most of the subject is therefore seen in shadow. This is relieved by the small, but intense, highlight in the middle of the frame, which attracts the eye and also prevents the image appearing flat and two-dimensional.

High contrast

IN PHOTOGRAPHIC TERMS, contrast refers to the exposure difference between the brightest highlight in a scene and the deepest shadow. This is relevant because both film and digital imaging chips are capable of recording subject detail in both of these parts of the frame only if the exposure difference is not too great. The contrast that they can 'see' without losing detail is far less than that which the human eye can deal with.

In general, it is reasonable to assume that a slow-to-medium film – say, ISO 200 – will be able to record a wider contrast range than a fast film of ISO 800. Similarly, film is generally slightly better at dealing with high contrast than digital devices.

In the images shown on these pages, the high-contrast results you can see are due to a variety of circumstances. In the building opposite, it is the tonal contrast of the subject itself, being composed of black against white. In the portrait, direct window light is reaching only one side of the subject's face, and so the other side is more in shadow. In the image below, the camera angle shows the subjects framed against a light, bright sky and so they appear as dark silhouettes. In each case, though, note how by using high contrast a real sense of impact has been imparted.

▲ Camera angle

A low camera angle looking up at the subjects shows them framed by a wide expanse of bright sky. By setting exposure for the brightest part of the scene, everything else has been reduced to a series of graphically powerful shapes. The foreground mud flats reflect light strongly, so they appear very bright.

HIGH CONTRAST

DIGITAL NOTES

• Some top-end digital cameras allow you to see a histogram showing the distribution of tones in a picture you have just taken. This not only can help you judge exposure, but shows the contrast range in the scene.

• Some cameras will even highlight areas within a scene that are too bright or too dark for any detail to be recorded (or rescued later).

▶ Window light

In this portrait of the author Agatha Christie the contrast on her face is obvious. A white cardboard reflector positioned on her shadow side was used, however, to return a little light and so prevent the difference in exposure from becoming too extreme.

▼ Black against white

The high contrast in this picture of an elegant Elizabethan building is the result of the stained-black woodwork seen against the white-painted walls.

High key and low key

TWO TYPES OF CONTRAST effect, known as high key and low key, use unusual tonal distributions to impart their own particular 'atmosphere'. In high key, the lighting produces tones that are predominantly light, with any dark areas occupying only a small area of the frame. The open, airy feeling given by a high-key picture is ideal for certain types of subject (*see right* and *below*). To reinforce high-key lighting, take your exposure reading from the darkest available area of the picture so that the aperture widens (or the time the shutter remains open lengthens).

A low-key picture is the opposite. In this type of picture, the lighting means that dark tones predominate and the type of atmosphere created is often dramatic, as you can see opposite. Any light tones or highlights should occupy only a small part of the picture area. To emphasize low-key lighting, take an exposure reading from the brightest area of the frame. In this way, the aperture will close down (or the length of time the shutter remains open will shorten) to provide a darker exposure.

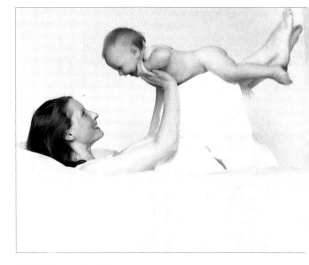

▲ Mother and child
Delicacy is one of the characteristics of a high-key picture. This scene of a mother and baby is flooded with light, matching the sunny expressions of the subjects.

▼ Hazy sunset
One of the effects of haze is that the dust particles in the atmosphere bounce the light around, making a high-key result relatively easy to achieve.

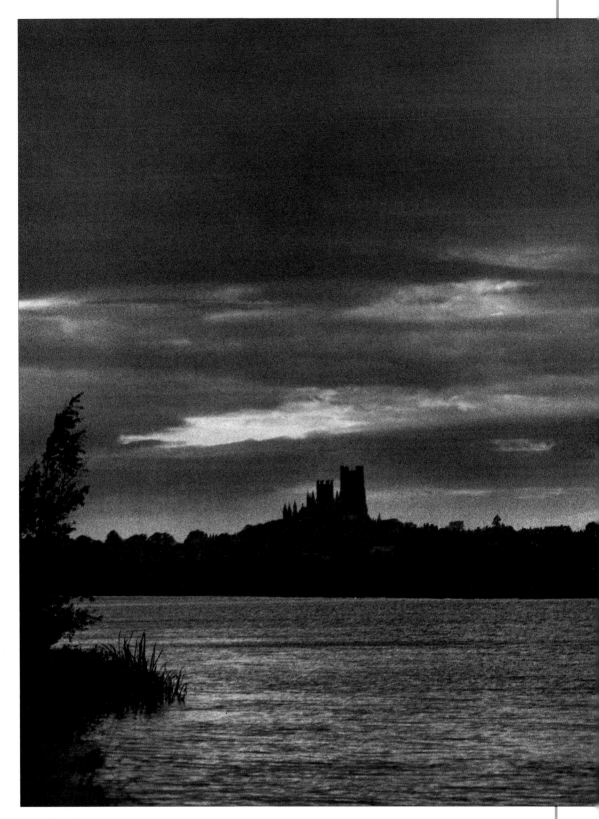

▲ Stormy light

A low-key interpretation of this scene is the perfect way to capture the brooding, slightly ominous quality of the castle on the far bank. The exposure reading was taken from the bright area of sky showing through the threatening storm clouds, and this caused the rest of the scene to underexpose to varying degrees.

Image grain

AT SOME STAGE OR ANOTHER you will hear photographers talking about 'grain'. The emulsion of a strip of film is made up of minute grains of a light-sensitive material, known as silver halides. It is the chemical change that takes place in the structure of these grains that makes up the image you see as a negative (or as a print).

In a slow film – anything up to about ISO 125 – the grains are small and densely packed. The result is that, when enlarged to a normal degree, the individual grains cannot be seen on the print. Such a result would be known as fine-grained. The emulsions of fast films, however – such as ISO 800 or higher – contain large grains

of silver halides. Large grains have a larger surface area and, thus, are more light sensitive. When enlarged the grains can show as a distinct pattern on some films. Chromogenic films (such as Ilford XP2) create an image on the final negative using dyes, rather than the silver itself, so the grain structure is less marked at high ISO ratings.

The appearance of grain is not always a disadvantage. Sometimes specific film developers are used to accentuate its appearance, or just a small part of a negative is enlarged in order to emphasize the grain pattern. You will also see from looking at the pictures on these pages that grain is always more apparent in the light-toned areas.

◀▼ Degrees of enlargement
These two images demonstrate how grain becomes more noticeable the greater the degree of enlargement. The version on the left is the scene of a Parisian metro entrance printed from the whole of an ISO 200 negative. The version below is a blow-up from a small part of the same negative. You can see immediately that the grain is much more pronounced. Note, too, that the grain is more obvious in some tones than it is in others.

DIGITAL NOTES

• Digital cameras allow you to alter the sensitivity of the imaging chip on a frame-by-frame basis. Although there is no grain, there is more noise in the image the higher the ISO setting. This has an appearance similar to grain.

• 'Artistic' grain can be added in the digital darkroom using standard one-step filters – or by over-sharpening using the Unsharp Mask (USM) utility.

▶ Speed enhancement

The ISO 400 negative that produced this print was developed in a special speed-enhancing developer. As a result, the grain response in parts of the image has taken on an almost tangible three-dimensional quality.

▼ Grain for effect

In this shot of a mine works, the pronounced grain helps conjure up an atmosphere of the degraded landscape associated with industrial areas.

Texture

ONCE YOU EXTRACT COLOUR from a scene, other surface characteristics of the subject assume greater importance. One of the most telling of these is texture, because it is the degree of roughness or smoothness of the subject that adds vital visual information and interest to a photograph. Surface texture also gives you the sense that the picture you are looking at has a tactile quality and so helps you to imagine what it would be like if you could reach out and actually touch whatever is depicted.

Texture becomes evident when light strikes the surface of your subject at a distinct angle, such as in the early morning or late afternoon when the sun is low in the sky and rakes across the field of view of your camera lens. This has the effect of illuminating the high points and casting shadows that leave the corresponding hollows, or low points, in darkness. With a portrait, moving in close can give the skin of your subject a three-dimensional reality; in a landscape, it can make you feel as if you could walk into the frame.

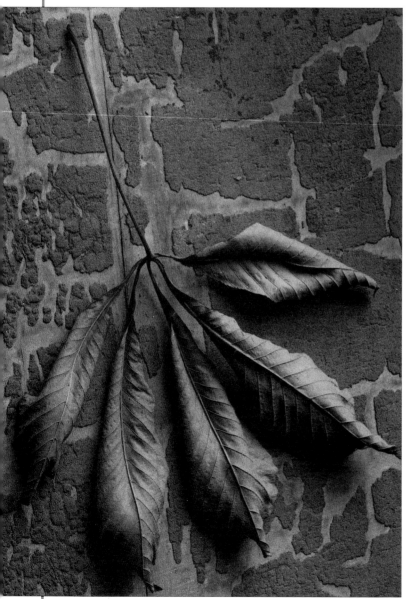

◄ Isolated detail
The low angle of the light in this still-life study illuminates only the highest surfaces of a dried and curling leaf, leaving pools of cool shadow that give it a very tactile quality. Note, too, how the roughness of the background has been accentuated.

TEXTURE

▲ Skin

The light for this close-up of the wrinkled hands of an 80-year-old man came from daylight entering the room through a small window. The directional quality of window light can cause problems of contrast (*see pp. 20–21*) in a more general portrait, but here the extreme difference between light and shadow produces a composition in which texture is the main subject.

▶ Emphasis through selection

By selecting just a small part of a large subject – here the undulating base of an enormous stone statue of Buddha – you can emphasize the texture that would otherwise have passed unnoticed if all the statue had been shown. Note how, as well as showing texture, the contrast between light and shade produces a sense of depth.

Leading the eye

WHEN LOOKING AT any photograph, we instinctively seek some sort of order in the visual information it contains. You can exploit this preference for order by selecting a camera angle and framing to give the strongest impression of your subject and to lead the viewer's eye through the image in a particular way.

Line, tone and perspective

One way of leading the viewer's eye is to link subject elements by lines occurring naturally in the scene, such as those created by a flight of steps and balustrade, for example, leading to something you wish to stress.

Tone can also be used to link different parts of the frame, with the eye using areas of similar tonal value to explore an image in much the same way as you would use stepping stones to navigate a course.

Perspective, too, is a device you can exploit, utilizing diminishing scale, converging parallel lines and overlapping forms to suggest a way of interpreting the image.

▼ **Eyeline**
The tendency when seeing a person looking at something, is to follow their gaze – a perfect way of directing the viewer's attention to another part of the frame.

▲ Tone and perspective

In this moorland image, a ribbon of silver leads the eye from the immediate foreground to the far distance. The apparent convergence of the lines of the river banks, which seem to draw you deeper into the frame, emphasizes the route our eyes should take.

▼ Curved lines

The dark edges marking the border between the lawns and the driveway gently lead your eye through the picture from the foreground, through the gate, and to the grand stately home behind.

THE COLLEGE OF WEST ANGLIA

Framing the subject

THE VISUAL CONTENT of a photograph can often be simplified and strengthened by choosing a camera angle that shows the main subject framed by other elements of the composition. Frames can be of many different types and often all you need do is shift your camera position until they and the subject align properly when seen through the camera's viewfinder or on the LCD preview screen.

Frames can be shown sharply focused, so forming an integral part of the composition. Alternatively, they can be soft and indistinct, and used largely to fill what would otherwise be an uninteresting part of the picture – such as an expanse of flat-toned sky or a distracting element in

the foreground. For the former effect, a combination of a wide-angle lens setting and a small aperture will usually render the frame in focus, assuming that it is not too close to the lens. For the latter effect, a longer focal length and a wide aperture will usually allow you to show the frame as a soft blur, especially if you position it close to the lens.

Tonal rendition

When working in colour, you need to take the colour of the frame into account to make sure it does not distract attention from the main subject. In black and white, however, your only concern is with its tonal value and whether it is sufficiently different so as not to merge with or confuse the subject.

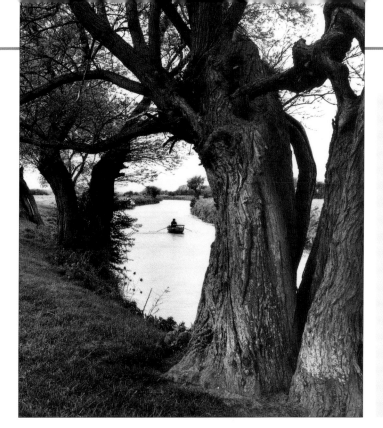

DIGITAL NOTES

• A digital camera's LCD viewfinder allows you to check your composition after you take a shot – as well as before. Use this facility to ensure horizons are level, and that there isn't anything in the frame that shouldn't be there.

• Use the magnification facility, if you have one, to check that the important parts of the picture you have just shot are in focus – and the distracting ones are adequately out of focus. You can then reshoot if the settings aren't quite right.

• LCDs are very hard to view in bright light. Find a shaded area, or carry a dark piece of material to use as a hood.

▲Sharply focused frame

In this example, the gracefully curving trunks of the near and distant tree meet to form a natural arch through which the subject can be seen. A 35mm wide-angle lens ·setting was used with an aperture of f11, showing the whole frame as equally sharp.

◄ Softly focused frame

In this view, a frame has been created by shooting through a clear area in the foreground foliage, which was almost touching the front of a 135mm lens. With the foliage this close to a long lens, an aperture of f16 was selected, in order to ensure the distant subject was sharply focused, in the full knowledge that the curtain of leaves and branches would appear almost transparently soft.

► Frames within frames

The frame of sacking material used in this picture has been integrated with the image of the subject. This light-hearted portrait shows the subject peering out through a slit in the material; his hands, widening the gap, form yet another frame around his face.

Unusual viewpoints

PHOTOGRAPHS OFTEN GAIN additional impact when they show the subject from an unusual viewpoint. Even if your first view of a subject is favourable, take the time and trouble to explore different camera angles and perspectives. For example, drop down on one knee so that you see the subject through the viewfinder from a lower-than-normal viewpoint. If a chair is available, try viewing your subject from an angle greater than normal eye-level, which is the height from which the overwhelming majority of shots are taken. If

you are shooting outdoors, a rigid-framed camera case makes a convenient shooting platform, giving you the advantage of a little extra height.

Unusual viewpoints can also be achieved by isolating just the crucial picture elements. Finding a camera position that strips away the clutter allows the viewer to concentrate on your perception of the scene. Try and pre-visualize how you will be able to improve the shot in the traditional or digital darkroom, by cropping or by removing unwanted elements in the scene.

▶ Offset elements

To produce this picture I had to shoot from a low angle. What I wanted to show were the nurse's anxious eyes toward the bottom of the frame and the object of her concern – the drip – at the extreme top. By offsetting and isolating the subject elements in this way, a tension is created as the viewer's eyes flick between the two.

◀ Depth of field

A low camera angle shows a doctor against a plain, non-distracting background. A 50mm lens, set at f2.8 and used closed up, ensures that only the doctor's hands and the test tube appear sharp in the image.

▼ Shooting down

To gain the height for this photograph, I climbed to the top rung of a tall stepladder and shot downward. This viewpoint makes it appear almost as if the powerful highlight shining on the studio floor is, in fact, the light source, and the model is somehow fixed to its outside surface.

Movement–recording action

THE MOST IMPORTANT camera control for recording subject movement and action is the shutter speed. The shutter control is calibrated in fractions of a second, such as 1/4000, 1/1000, 1/250, 1/60, 1/15, and so on all the way down to very long exposure times of a full second or more. Traditionally each shutter speed either halves or doubles the length of time the shutter remains open – although intermediate speeds are also available on some cameras.

When deciding which shutter speed to set, you need to take two things into account. First, can the shutter speed be compensated for by an appropriate aperture to ensure correct exposure? If you were to set 1/2 sec on a bright, sunny day, then even the smallest aperture available, and the slowest ISO setting on a digital camera, may result in overexposure. Conversely, if the light levels are poor, a shutter exposure of 1/2000 sec may give underexposure even with the widest aperture.

Second, the length of time the shutter is open determines how a moving subject appears in the image. If you were to set a slow shutter speed – say, 1/30 sec – to record a speeding car, it is likely to appear streaked and blurry (unless the camera is panned). This may be just the impressionistic effect you want. Changing to a shutter speed of 1/2000 sec with the same subject, however, would almost certainly result in a sharp, frozen image – giving an entirely different type of image.

▼ **Fast flash**
Flash light gives an extremely brief, intense burst of light, fast enough to 'freeze' the movement of the liquid in the bowl when an ice cube is dropped into it. When using flash in a restricted space in low light, the shutter speed is almost incidental.

DIGITAL NOTES

• There is a delay between firing the shutter and the picture being taken on all cameras. But this 'shutter lag' can be particularly long on some digital cameras – as the system needs time to boot up before taking the shot. This delay varies significantly from model to model.

• Digital cameras also need time to write the data to memory after taking a shot. This can restrict the number of shots that can be taken in quick succession.

▶ **White water**
The speed and unpredictability of a canoeist swept along through a series of rapids requires a fast shutter speed if you want to ensure a recognizable image. The shutter speed used here was 1/500 sec.

▼ **Movement across the frame**
Freezing movement across the frame needs a faster shutter speed than movement at 45° or directly toward or away from the camera. To stop the motorcyclist in mid-air like this, a shutter speed of 1/1000 sec was used.

▲ Panning

To capture the speed and excitement of this cycle race the camera's shutter speed was set to 1/30 sec and the camera panned. This involves swinging the camera round while the shutter is open to keep pace with the subject. This has given a sharp image of the cyclists while rendering all stationary objects as a series of streaks.

▼ Camera movement

Unless you are panning, you will usually want to keep the camera completely still to avoid camera shake. However, in this example you can see how the slightly soft image produced by camera movement has given a real sense of excitement and action to the image of horsemen thundering by.

DIGITAL NOTES

• Digital cameras allow you to achieve very fast and very slow shutter speeds more easily than with film cameras – as you can change the ISO rating on a shot-by-shot basis.

• To achieve very slow shutter speeds in daylight, it may be necessary to fit a neutral density (ND) filter over the lens, to restrict the amount of light entering the camera. This technique can also be used with film cameras.

◄ Slow shutter speed

One way of recording movement is to set a slow shutter speed on a solidly supported camera and so allow the subject to record as a streaky, blurry image, while all fixed or unmoving elements of the scene record sharply.

Filters

COLOURED FILTERS ARE frequently used with black and white film to help clearly differentiate the tonal values of colours, or to change the mood or atmosphere of a picture by either lightening or darkening its tones overall. As a general rule, a filter will normally lighten the tone of any colour corresponding to its own and it may also darken other tones. To preview the type of effect a filter will have, hold it to your eye.

Much deeper coloured filters are used with black and white film than are usually used with colour stock. This is because the colour of the filter will selectively lighten or darken the tonal equivalents of colours, rather than producing an overall cast corresponding to the colour of the filter used on the lens.

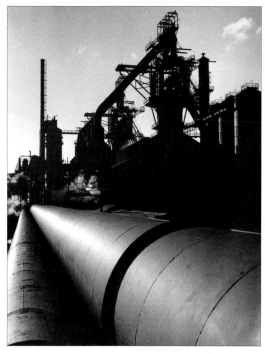

▼ Yellow filter
A deep yellow filter has been used here to darken the grey tone corresponding to the area of blue sky and so help to give the clouds slightly better definition.

▲ Green filter
As well as making the sky appear slightly darker, a green filter has been used to darken the tones created by the red pipes in the foreground of this shot.

B&W FILTER EFFECTS

• Blue filter (Wratten 47): lightens areas of blue; darkens reds, oranges and yellows.

• Green filter (Wratten 58): lightens green areas; darkens blues, oranges and reds.

• Yellow filter (Wratten 8): lightens areas of yellow, orange and red; darkens blues.

• Orange filter (Wratten 16): lightens areas of orange and red; darkens blues and greens.

• Red filter (Wratten 25): lightens red; darkens blues and greens.

▶ Red filter

A red filter has the most dramatic effect on skies, making them appear very dark and forbidding. It has no effect on white clouds, however, and so produces a very contrasty effect. It also makes vegetation appear very dark toned. If you underexpose by about two stops when using a red filter, daylight scenes appear as if they were shot by moonlight.

DIGITAL NOTES

• Although coloured filters can be used successfully to create black and white images with a digital camera, they are not widely used.

• It is easier, and you can exercise more control, if the image is shot in full colour. Then, in the digital darkroom, you can produce black and white conversions which emulate the effect of using coloured filters by mixing the colour channels in different proportions, and by darkening and lightening different hues (see *pages 150–151*).

◀ Orange filter

An orange filter noticeably darkens the tones of a pale blue sky while leaving clouds unaffected. The effect is not as strong, however, as when using a red filter.

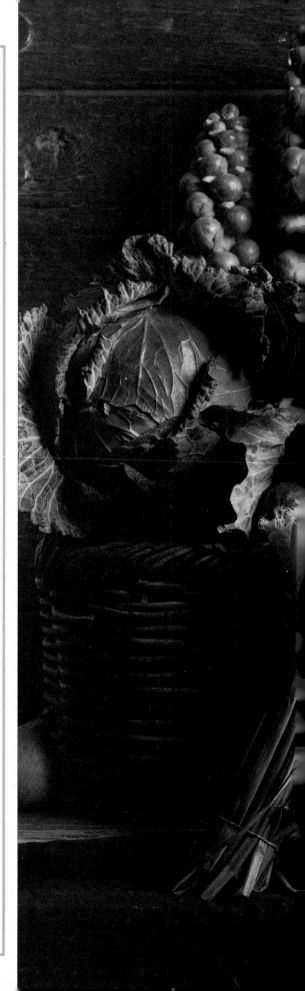

Still lifes

A CAREFUL AND methodical approach is the prerequisite for consistently good still-life photographs. Unlike sports and action photography, where you must grab your shots almost by reflex, or even landscape photography, which is dependent on the fickleness of weather conditions and the ever-changing patterns of light and shade, in still-life photography you normally have the luxury of time.

Use this time to make sure that every element of the composition is exactly right: check that the lighting angles will illuminate the appropriate areas of the composition and suppress others; ensure that your camera position and lens focal length are precisely set to show everything to best advantage. Then, finally, check everything again through the viewfinder before taking the shot.

Good still-life pictures don't rely on expensive or complicated lighting equipment – particularly when shooting in black and white. Most often you can make do with ordinary sunlight, diffused if necessary to soften its effect. Add a few simple reflectors made of white cardboard or kitchen foil to relieve over-dense shadows, and use a basic flashgun to add a highlight. The rest is imagination.

▶ **Find a theme**
It is the obvious connection between the elements in this still life that makes it such a satisfying composition. The illumination is directional window light with a little fill-in provided by two cardboard reflectors.

Creating a still-life picture

Having decided on a theme for your still-life photograph, the first step is to gather together all the potential elements that could be included in the composition. Ideally you will want to have more objects available than are eventually used, in order to give yourself some flexibility with the design and a variety of shots.

The next step is to decide where you want your still-life objects set up. If you are reliant principally on window light, then a shelf or table top close to your light source will be required. If, however, you are using flash or tungsten lighting, or a mixture of these – remember, there are no colour casts to worry about with black and white –

then you will have more options to consider; in this case, let the availability of an appropriate background sway your decision.

Now, with the camera on a tripod, you can start arranging your objects. In general, it helps to place the largest one first, but not necessarily in centre frame, however; off-centre placement often gives more vitality and makes the remainder of the available space easier to work with.

Every time you add an object, or alter the lighting, go back to the camera and check how it looks through the viewfinder. Then, for maximum sharpness, set the smallest aperture and fire the shutter with a cable release or delayed timer.

CREATING A STILL-LIFE PICTURE

▶ Window light

This simple still-life composition is lit solely by window light from the left of the jug and teapot, and much of the interest in the shot lies in the clearly demarcated blocks of light and shade. It is the small details that are so often important, and here you can see that it is the black enamelled rims of these objects that help pull them away from the background, increasing the feeling of depth and distance.

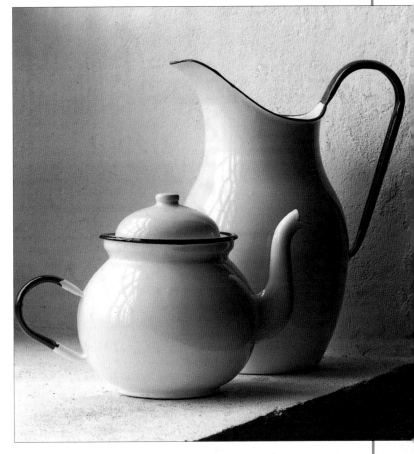

◀ Studio flash

This still-life composition is lit by contrasty and very directional studio flash set to the right of the group of containers. This has produced a strongly textural image in which you can almost reach out and feel the surface of the wicker and the hard undulating surfaces of the walnuts, brazils and hazelnuts.

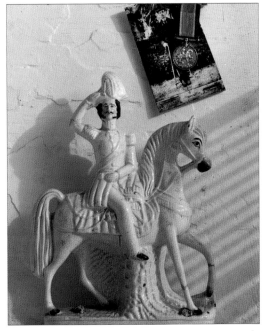

▲ Daylight and tungsten

These shots introduce the concept of 'visual weight'. The underlit figure (*above left*), shot with window light, has a heavy, substantial feel. Compare this with the next shot (*above right*), which, with the addition of tungsten lamps, is more delicate but also more all-revealing; as a result, it loses some of its sense of mystery.

Aesthetic arrangements

THE POTENTIAL SUBJECT MATTER for still-life compositions is so broad that it can be difficult to know where to make a start. One way to work is to limit your choice of subject elements to things that all have some obvious connection with each other. This connection could be a hobby or activity, such as golf, and the subject elements could then comprise clubs, balls, tees, spiked shoes, and so on. Equally, you could select utensils used in the kitchen as the building blocks for a still life, or a disparate collection of objects that are connected merely by their shape, the material from which they are made, or their age.

In a small-scale still-life composition, in which the objects are easily countable, you will generally find that it is easier to make an aesthetic arrangement out of an uneven number of subject elements. Another advantage of starting small is that the lighting scheme is easier to manage, as there are fewer problems with distracting shadows.

▶ Culinary composition

It is important to confine attention to the components making up the image. Take any of the elements out of this group and the sense of balance and harmony, of form and function, would be disturbed.

▼ Period piece

In this arrangement, all the components come from a bygone age. Images of people predominate, looking as if they have burst out of the chest of drawers around which the composition is based.

▲ Autumnal theme

The subjects here are the spiny-cased fruit of the horse chestnut tree. One has been released and is threaded for a game of 'conkers', and the leather thong forms a boundary within which the other elements are confined.

Still life to tell a story

I F YOU HAVE A PARTICULAR interest in a historical character, then a little research might reveal a museum with a collection of interesting memorabilia that you could photograph. If you are lucky there may also be, as in the case of Robert Burns, who is the subject of these pictures, a national monument you could visit. Contacting one of the historical societies you will find listed in the telephone book, or the relevant local tourist authority, is probably your best starting point for this type of information.

All of these pictures were taken at Robert Burns' birthplace, in a cottage in Alloway, near Ayr in Scotland. As well as a still life showing a group of items used by Burns and likenesses of this great poet, there are also smaller groups showing certain objects in detail. To shoot these, it was necessary to obtain the permission of the curator and pay a small fee to have them moved into the best positions for photography.

Because the cottage remained open to the public throughout, it was not possible to set up artificial lights. This made it essential to visit the day before to discover the best time of day for natural daylight and also to see when the cottage was likely to be least used.

▼ Personal insights

Still lifes like these make it much easier to think of Burns as an actual person rather than just a historical personality. In these compositions, manuscripts have been grouped together with personal items such as his pipe, and there is a silhouetted likeness propped up against a songbook of Burns' preferred lyrics of 'Auld Lang Syne'. These have been poignantly linked to the image of his shaving mirror and cut-throat razor, which looks a little like the hands of a broken clock.

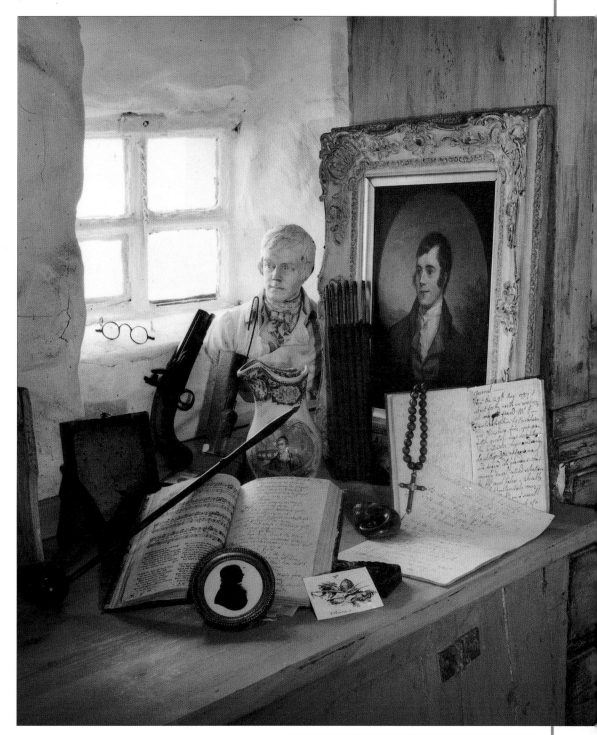

▲ Using a tripod

Although it was not possible to use studio-type lighting in Burns' cottage, a tripod was permitted. Luckily, the old glass in the window behind was not of today's high standards and so it rather softened and diffused the overcast light as it passed through. This was enough, with the use of a fold-away gold-coloured reflector, to give a very satisfactory even lighting. The composition was then shot with a 50mm lens stopped down to f16 and a shutter speed of 1 ½ seconds.

DIGITAL NOTES

• When using a tripod with a long exposure you need to avoid vibrations caused by pressing the shutter button, which will affect the sharpness of the picture. Although a cable release can be used with some cameras, it is often easier to use the self-timer control, which will fire the shutter after a two- or ten-second delay.

'Found' still lifes

NOT ALL STILL LIFE photographs are set up in the studio or on a table top. If you take the time to look, you will find that your own home, and the streets you walk down every day, are full of still-life photo opportunities.

Some 'found' still-life studies result from our innate sense of design – ornaments arranged on a shelf are an expression of our desire to make our surroundings more pleasant, for example, and such

a group could make a perfect still-life picture.

Other found still lifes occur through the association of objects used in a particular task – an arrangement of utensils, for example, placed so that they come easily to hand when required. Shop windows are another source of images. You may, however, have only limited control over lighting and you will have to work hard to find the right angle to show your subject in isolation.

▲ Gardening shoes
Tucked against a wall near the back door, these gardening shoes were been slipped off, some laces still tied, before their owners entered the house. When isolated by the camera like this, such ordinary objects can make an ideal composition.

◄ Wait for the light
The simplicity of the objects making up this still life has an immediate appeal. When first seen, however, the light was frontal and any sense of texture was absent. Three hours later, the sun had moved around and dropped lower in the sky, and the character of the objects was totally transformed.

▶ Repeating pattern
By tightly framing just a section of this neatly stacked pile of terracotta pipes, it was possible to create a still-life composition with almost rigid uniformity of shape and form.

Portraits

O F ALL THE AREAS of photographic interest, pictures of people – portraits – are the ones we most readily identify with. We study the subject's face, whether that person is known to us or not, trying to discern in the eyes, the set of the face, something of their inner thoughts, character and motivations. In a fuller-length portrait, in which the face is perhaps not shown in that much detail, we interpret the body language instead and look at the subject in relation to the other picture elements, again in an almost automatic attempt to try to understand something about that person.

Successful portrait photography is, therefore, concerned not only with the person who represents the main focus of attention in a picture, but also with all the other areas of the frame.

Before taking any picture, look at all of the frame. Decide what you want to include or omit, adjust the lens focal length or the camera position and determine the most appropriate shutter speed and aperture. Then – and only then – press the shutter release.

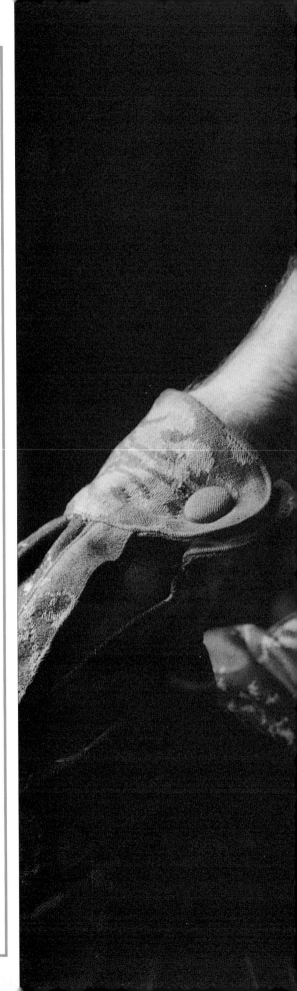

▶ **Character close-up**
This arresting portrait of Welsh photographer Angus McBean shows very simply the flamboyance and ease of a man best known for the extravagance and originality of his own photographic style – which often involved the building of elaborate sets, double exposures and various montage effects.

Capturing personality

THERE ARE MANY varied aspects of portrait photography – formal portraits, candid shots, children, nudes and glamour, and so on – and each is concerned, primarily, with different facets of the subject. For any one of these types of portrait to be successful, however, the image has to communicate at some level with the viewer and, for this to happen, something of the subject's personality must be clearly recorded by the camera. This is the art of portrait photography.

Weighting the odds

You will greatly increase the chances of a successful portrait session if you build some sort of rapport with your subject. This is more than important, it is vital! Before the session starts,

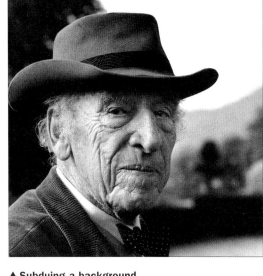

▲ Subduing a background

This series of photographs is of the architect Clough Williams-Ellis, builder of the Italianate fantasy village of Portmeirion on the coast of Wales. The village and its grounds were used as the setting, but in this shot, a long 135mm lens and an aperture of f4 ensure that the distant landscape is reduced to an impressionistic blur, which gives just sufficient information without taking attention away from the rock-steady gaze and barely suppressed smile of the subject.

▲ Camera angle

This slightly high camera angle, looking down on the subject, has caused some foreshortening, something that I used here to emphasize the precision and style that so characterizes every aspect of the subject's personality and appearance.

▶ The grand tour

Asking the architect to show me around his creation was the perfect way of helping him to relax and enjoy the photo session. Here he pauses and turns, perfectly aligned between the shrubbery.

find some common areas of interest, and continue talking to your subject while the session proceeds. Take lots of shots, varying framing between close-ups and full-lengths, look for less obvious shooting angles and make sure that the backgrounds contribute something positive to the images.

Working in black and white, you won't have to worry about the colour of the background or any other subject elements, but their tonal strength is an equally important consideration. So too is their degree of sharpness or blur, controlled by focal length and aperture. If your subject is dressed in light-coloured clothes, for example, he or she may look better against a dark-toned setting. And if this setting forms an important part of the shot, make sure that it is sharp, or at least reasonably so. If it is not important, then knock it out of focus.

▲ Showing the setting

In this shot of the architect Clough Williams-Ellis I wanted to show him framed by some of the buildings and garden architecture of his creation, Portmeirion. To do this, I used a 28mm wide-angle lens and an aperture of f16 to give a generous depth of field. It is interesting to note the pipe he is holding. It appears in all shots in which his hands are visible, and he held it unconsciously all the time, like a prop, to help himself relax.

▶ Framing the face

Character is always more obvious in a detailed close-up and the subtle tonal gradation in this photograph is the type of effect that attracts many people to the black and white medium. The light grey of his hat not only frames his head perfectly, but it also helps to separate him from the background, bringing the figure forward in the frame.

Using props

PHOTOGRAPHIC PROPS can enrich your portrait photographs. Often they are used by photographers to help add information about their subjects and so produce a more rounded, 'fleshed-out' portrait. This type of picture most often emerges when subjects are photographed where they work or live, and so the setting will be full of things relevant to what they do, their homes or how they spend their time.

If the subject of your portrait is ill at ease or uncomfortable about the presence of the camera, then props can come to your assistance simply by providing a focus for the subject's attention. Although the prop may be serving no purpose other than giving them something to do with their hands (*see p. 53*), it still could be saying something about them in a more oblique fashion. Take care, however, since too much detail may be distracting and weaken the photograph's impact.

▲ Garden prop
The spade and fork slung over the shoulder of this old gentleman are rather obvious props but they help to give a proper context to the subject. Other areas of the frame – such as the glasshouse in the background and the massive pile of pruned branches stacked just behind him, their contorted shapes echoing his bent legs and back – reinforce this.

▶ Musical notes
For this shot of a conductor at work with his orchestra I deliberately chose a camera angle where the musical scores of the string players would create the foreground of the picture. The lines of musical notes on the open pages immediately set the scene for the portrait.

▲ Incidental props

In this portrait of sculptor Elizabeth Frink we see her in the garden of her studio. The photograph is framed so that approximately half the image is taken up with a row of sculpted heads set on tall concrete pedestals.

It is the position of the head on the far left, however, which is most significant. It seems to be staring directly at its creator, thus helping to fix the viewer's attention where it is intended to go.

Choosing a background

RATHER THAN BEING a neutral backcloth to the main action, the background of a portrait demands as much care and attention as any other area of the frame. Poor backgrounds distract from the picture of the sitter, or give a misleading idea about his or her lifestyle.

Backgrounds are most often thought of as acting in some sort of subsidiary role in a photograph, as that part of the picture area against which you view the main subject. In the shots on these pages, however, you can see that the backgrounds have in fact been fully integrated and they are as vital to the subject matter as any other element, producing a richness and visual complexity that is compelling.

▼ Fantasy femmes

Perched on top of a drum of industrial-strength hand cleaner, this motor mechanic strikes a rather clichéd figure surrounded by the tools of his trade and an array of girlie posters on the wall behind.

CHOOSING A BACKGROUND

▶ Stressing the background
In this photograph, taken in a back-street in Rome, nearly all the visual information is contained within a single plane – the background. Even the figure of the young woman leaning in the doorway has become simply another background element.

▼ Camera angle
This picture was taken from a high camera angle, looking down on the subject. As a result, the figure is seen surrounded by tall crops. The tonal uniformity of the scene, consisting entirely of lighter shades of grey and white, produces an image dominated by shape and repeating pattern.

Using the environment

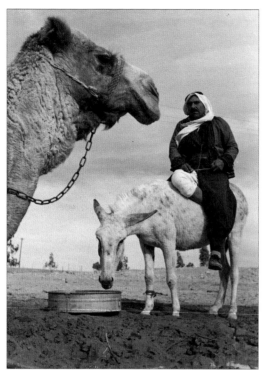

A MISTAKE MANY PHOTOGRAPHERS make is to concentrate so much of their attention on what they know to be the main subject of the picture that they fail to take account of the environment in which that subject will appear. Rather than being merely extraneous clutter, the environment in which you choose to show your subject is often what makes the picture interesting or unique.

Different ways of seeing

It does take some practice to be able to see, in your mind's eye, the way the subject and setting will relate to each other in a photograph. For a start, when you look at any scene your eyes constantly flick and dart as your attention is first caught by one thing, and then another. In this way you build up a complex, yet piecemeal impression in which some things are clearly defined while others – those that didn't interest you – are largely ignored and therefore suppressed. The camera, however, is not capable of making

▲ Leading the eye

With the largely arid flatness of a desert environment to contend with, you need to look for other subject elements to bring into play. Here, the camera position was intentionally selected to include the neck and head of the camel in the foreground. Not only does it lead your eye directly to the dark-clothed figure perched casually on the donkey's back, but also the difference in scale between the camel and man introduces a touch of humour.

▶ Atmospheric blur

This poorly lit indoor setting meant using a shutter speed too slow to freeze the movement of the potter's assistant, whose job it is to turn the wheel by hand. The neatly stacked pots between the women's heads are the fruits of their labour and the camera angle is sufficiently wide to show the primitive conditions in which they have to work.

▲ Wash day

This elderly couple lived all their lives happily on the land, enduring conditions that most city folk would find intolerable. The use of black and white film has increased that feeling of looking back in time and every part of the scene provides a wealth of information about a lifestyle that has largely ceased to exist – including a wood-burning boiler with a sooty chimney stack, wicker clothes basket, and hand-operated mangle.

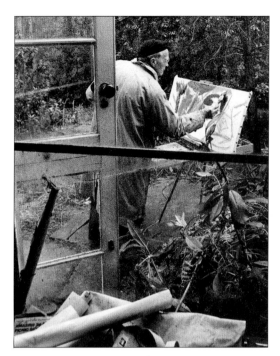

such sophisticated distinctions and, consequently, gives all subject elements much the same prominence – unless, of course, you take a hand.

The most effective way of pre-visualizing the finished photograph is to look at the scene through the camera's viewfinder. The hard edges of the viewfinder, especially of a digital camera's LCD screen, completely exclude detail other than that which will appear within the picture area. This is very different from the way you normally see a scene. With the camera to your eye, look at all four edges of the frame and see how even quite small shifts to the left or right, up or down, bring new elements into the scene, while others slide out of view. Adopting a low camera angle and shooting upward minimizes a less-than-attractive foreground, and shooting down from a high angle lessens the intrusion of more distant subject elements.

▲ Repeated shapes
This garden environment is an ideal setting for the English painter Ivon Hitchens, who is best known for his semi-abstract interpretations of broad landscape scenes. The edges of the door and the glazing bar seem almost to act as frames, echoing the strongly horizontal shape of the canvas.

◄ Precarious balance
A rather eccentric portrait of the painter Stanley Spencer perched precariously on a high stool while working on a large canvas tells us much about this artist's environment and method of working.

▶ Creative confusion
Sculptor Eduardo Paolozzi appears here to need the help of a stepladder in order to raise himself above the clutter and confusion of his studio. Although obviously a candid portrait, the camera angle has carefully picked out the only path through the sculpted figures and found a relatively clear area of floor leading to the subject himself.

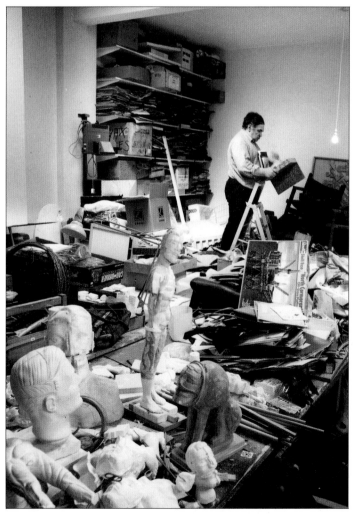

People at work

WHEN PEOPLE ARE AT WORK, and occupied with their duties, they are likely to forget the presence of the camera. This can work to your advantage, giving you the chance to capture relaxed and informal candid pictures.

If you know the type of area you will be shooting in – the amount of space available to move around in and likely light levels – you will then know the sort of lens that will be required, and whether artificial light will be necessary. In cramped conditions, a super-wide-angle lens, or wide-angle adaptor, may be needed. Adequate window light may mean you can shoot images without a tripod by using a fast film or a high ISO setting.

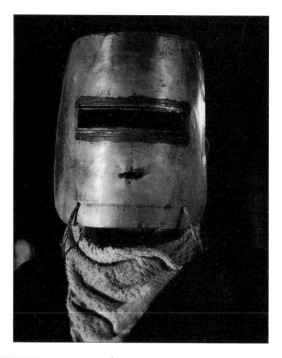

▼ Space-age close-up
The shots on these pages were taken in a foundry. This shot of a worker in full protective clothing and mask looks as if it comes from the set of a sci-fi movie.

◄ Showing the environment

Shots taken with a long lens are great for details, but the foundry environment I was shooting in was so dramatic that the only way to give a true indication of the place was to switch to the widest lens setting available for some of the pictures. Here we see the fully protected foundryman using a long rod to clear the channel along which the molten metal will run. The light being thrown out by the furnace was so intense that it illuminated the rest of the room.

▲ Look for frames

Frames (*see pp. 30–31*) can be used, as here, to help give a focus of attention to a photograph. By using some of the machinery as a frame for the subject I was also able to show interesting aspects of the workplace.

Informal portraits

PORTRAITS TAKEN WHEN the subject is relaxed and off guard can be most revealing. The trick here is either to draw your subject out, so that he or she starts to act naturally in front of the camera, or to go for a candid type of approach, where the subject is totally unaware of the camera's presence.

With either approach, a telephoto zoom is a most useful lens. If you are trying for candid shots, you will want as much distance between yourself and the subject as possible, without sacrificing too much in terms of image size. Use a lens setting of about 200mm, but take care that the shutter speed is fast enough to avoid any problems with camera shake. Even if your subject is a willing participant, you will need to get uncomfortably close to fill the frame with just the head and shoulders using anything less than a 90mm lens. If forced to use a shorter lens, pull back a little and enlarge the relevant part of the image later, on the computer screen or under the darkroom enlarger.

▲ Find a location
One approach to candid photography is to find a likely location, such as the public bath house in this shot taken in India, and wait for the subjects to come to you. I had already pre-focused the lens and set the exposure before the mother and son even entered. All that was necessary was to bring the camera up quickly and shoot when I judged the time to be right.

◄ Street location
In portraiture, unless the background makes a positive contribution, try to minimize its impact. In this street portrait, I used a 100mm lens to restrict the angle of view and an aperture of f5.6 to ensure that the background was unsharp.

► Studio location
This portrait of the English novelist J B Priestley was taken during a break in a portrait session. He was off guard and not expecting me to turn and shoot, and therefore he looks very relaxed.

Babies and children

CHILDREN CHANGE SO RAPIDLY – from babies to toddlers and then toddlers to teenagers. Without the camera to record our memories, so much would become hazy over the years.

The occasional formal portrait might be good for recognition but a more relaxed, candid approach often produces the best results, showing character as well as a likeness. Children's moods fluctuate wildly, so stay alert to any photo opportunities; don't concentrate only on 'happy snaps' – the sad moments can be just as telling.

In terms of film ISO setting, you may need to strike a balance between a fine-grain response, which is usually best for child portraits, and enough speed for a fast shutter speed to freeze any subject movement. An ISO 400 film or faster is essential for non-flash shots taken indoors.

▶ **Playing to the camera**
A shutter speed of 1/125 sec produces just enough blur to separate these daredevil stunt riders from a slightly streaky background.

BABIES AND CHILDREN

◄ Formal portrait
This charming portrait shows three children from the same family, and the high-key lighting approach is perfect for their young, fresh faces and blond hair. During printing, the centre of the negative, containing the image of the children, was printed through a circular hole in a piece of cardboard. This prevented light from the enlarger reaching the outside parts of the paper, which show up as white after development. A similar vignetted effect can easily be recreated in the digital darkroom.

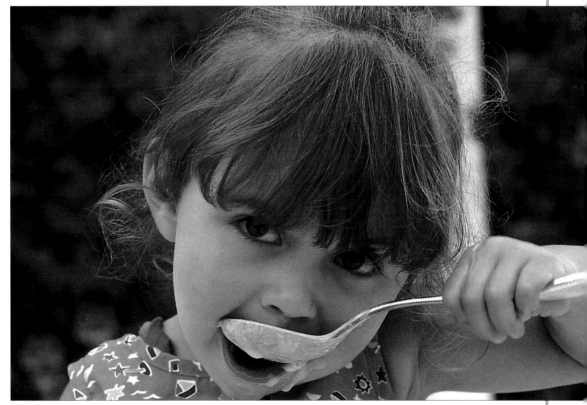

◄ Long lens
Lost in his own thoughts, this boy was photographed with a 250mm lens. If you are careful, this sort of telephoto focal length allows a detailed close-up without the subject ever being aware of your presence.

▲ Unposed portraits
Young children do not have a long attention span, so posed pictures must be taken quickly if you are to avoid tears and tantrums. But if a child is distracted, it is possible to shoot pictures for longer periods without complaint, and without them walking off. In this shot, the girl is so engrossed in eating her ice cream that I was able to take a sequence of successful pictures. Unposed portraits may well provide more typical poses and expressions than a formal portrait sitting.

Hands and feet

APART FROM THE FACE, hands are probably the most informative and expressive parts of the body. Hand movements and gestures, and the way hands are held when relaxed or excited, are a vital part of the communication process, and it is interesting to note that they are very rarely completely still. The way we conduct our lives may also often be evident in our hands – the condition of the skin and nails, lines, creases and folds. When seen up close, people's hands can seem like contour maps of their lives.

An unusual portrait approach is to concentrate on the hands or feet of your subject. If you are taking the photographs for your own use, then there is no overriding reason to produce pictures that are instantly recognizable as being of a particular person, and people's hands and feet can often be very revealing of character and lifestyle.

Feet are a neglected part of the anatomy. For the most part encased in socks or shoes, once revealed and isolated by the camera they can make fascinating abstract forms to photograph.

◀ Lenses and lighting
For a close-up like this, it is best to take a camera position back from the subject and then use a long lens to bring the hands up to full-frame size. If you move in too close with the camera, it makes positioning the lighting that much more difficult, since either you or your equipment may cast unwanted shadows over the subject.

▶ Abstract images
The very tight framing of this photograph has effectively isolated the subject's feet. When seen like this, stacked on top of each other, they take on a rather sculptural quality and appear almost as abstract images. The lighting was directional to ensure that there were areas of shadow to contrast with the brighter, highlighted parts.

▲ Depth of field

Hands are very revealing – compare those of a manual worker, for example, with those of an artist and you can see their different histories laid before you. The hand of this subject has not been framed to isolate it physically from the rest of his body. Instead, the lens was focused on his hand and then a wide lens aperture selected to ensure that the more distant parts of his body would be recorded only as a much softened, out-of-focus background that would provide interest without actually competing for attention.

The male nude

J UST AS THE tonal range of black and white imaging can be used to excellent effect to express the rounded forms and fine-textured qualities of the female form, so too can it be used with equal success to show the power and grace of the male body – this is an often neglected aspect of nude photography.

Lighting

The best principal light source for the human figure is undoubtedly diffused sidelighting – from a window, flash or tungsten units, or a combination of any of these. One of the attributes of sidelighting in portraiture is that it accentuates the skin texture of your subject and, with a male subject, this will help to emphasize the coarser skin texture that is associated with male as compared with female subjects. Pictures of the male nude, however, often benefit from higher levels of contrast than you would normally use for female nudes. The lighting scheme is essentially simplified, since there is less need for fill-in lighting and reflectors, a single sidelight often being all that is needed.

Directing your subject to adopt the right pose will help to show particular muscle groups in his body. By using appropriate zoom settings and framing, you can then isolate these to create fascinating semi-abstract images.

THE MALE NUDE

◀ Cropping for emphasis
Using a telephoto lens setting will isolate part of the subject's body. The detail here shows the well-developed muscle groups in the small of this model's back and buttocks. These features have been emphasized by the use of body oil, which increase the tonal contrast between the high spots and hollows. Note, too, the obvious skin texture resulting from the use of very directional sidelighting.

▶ The right pose
For this shot I asked the subject to clasp his hands behind his head in order to set up the right muscle tension in his upper arms, shoulders and back. At the last second I also asked him to shift his weight slightly on to his right leg. This made the pose look more relaxed and natural and it also created that interesting fold of skin and muscle on the right-hand side of his waist.

◀ Using fill-in light
This picture reveals a softer approach to lighting. Although the main light is still sidelighting, positioned on the far side of the subject and shining at about 45°, some frontal light has also been added to reduce contrast. The power of his figure is still evident, but his form looks predominantly rounded, and there is a softer, more yielding quality to his figure in marked contrast to his tightly clenched hands.

The human form

DEPENDING ON HOW you light and pose your model, photographs of nudes can take on a clinical explicitness, concentrate more on such qualities as form, texture, shape and pattern, or use more atmospheric and expressive compositions that include the setting, too.

Lighting effects

Unless you have access to a studio, the most readily available light source is daylight. And because of the obvious difficulties of privacy involved in photographing a nude outside on location, you will probably be restricted to an indoor setting, using window light.

The directional qualities of window light, which often create problems of excessive contrast in normal portraiture, can work in your favour when dealing with the human form. Pockets of shadow, in which detail is completely lacking, may help to produce a more abstract result, especially if you move in close, use a long lens, or crop the image in the digital or traditional darkroom, to exclude parts of the figure.

If, however, you want a more tonally consistent result, you can always introduce a reflector, flash lighting or, indeed, domestic tungsten room lighting – perhaps from an adjustable desk lamp – in order to reduce contrast in selected parts of the subject. Another way of creating a more generalized, softer type of light is to cover the window with net curtains or tracing paper to diffuse and spread the light entering the room.

◀ **Window light**
Posing the model against the wall gives a neutral backdrop to this shot. The pattern of light and shade, cast by the slats of the venetian blinds over the window, creates a strongly abstract image in which sexuality is suppressed in favour of pattern. This abstract quality is emphasized by the tight cropping of the subject, which excludes her head and legs.

▶ **Emphasizing form**
The use of a wide-angle lens positioned close in has elongated the apparent length of the model's arm. Also, photographic tungsten light angled so that her head is swallowed up in deep shadow, and the pose showing her body folded over on itself, combine to produce a composition in which form is the principal feature.

▲ Emphasizing form

With female nudes, you will generally want to use softer sidelighting than when photographing males (see page 70). By using diffuse lighting to the side of the model, you can create enough shadow areas to provide a suggestion of three-dimensional form. But you want to avoid making shadows areas that are so harsh that the subtlety of the body's curves, and the delicateness of the skin's texture, are lost. In this sepia shot, the lighting is provided by natural light through a window, diffused using a suspended white sheet.

Abstracting the nude

MOVING IN VERY CLOSE to the subject, in order to fill the frame with isolated parts of the anatomy, can turn the human body into a landscape of pictorial possibilities.

The lighting of a detail, such as those you can see on these pages, is not dissimilar to that required for a full figure. The main characteristics you will probably want to emphasize are outline shape, form and surface qualities. The best place to position your lights to achieve this is somewhere on an arc starting with the light virtually parallel to the subject, giving a racking effect, to about three-quarters on.

To help you plan your composition, use the camera's viewfinder constantly to check exactly the view as seen by the lens. When looking directly at your subject, without the aid of the lens, your eyes take in too much of the surrounding detail that will not form part of the final picture.

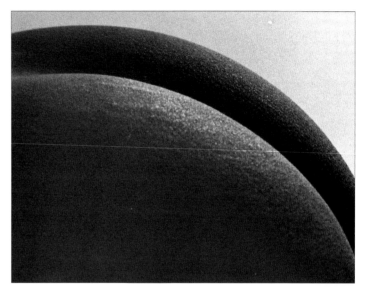

▶ Repeating shapes
In this close-up, the camera angle and lighting have isolated the subject's buttocks. The perfect symmetry of the repeating curves is strengthened by a light set to just graze the topmost surfaces, providing a contrast with the deep shadow between.

◀ Seascape
Looking like the gently undulating surface of a moonlit seascape, this intriguing close-up shows an isolated part of the abdomen, with the skin pushed into tight folds by the subject's pose.

▶ Opportunity strikes
The opportunity for this picture occurred on a coffee break during a normal shoot, when I noticed the male model I was using absent-mindedly massaging the skin on his upper chest with his thumb.

Studio lighting

DON'T BE PUT OFF when you hear the word 'studio', thinking that you need a professional kit of expensive lights and masses of space. Even a small spare room can be used as a temporary studio. For lighting you can rely solely on daylight, or a mixture of daylight, a flashgun, ordinary domestic lights such as adjustable desk lamps, and a few cardboard reflectors.

If you do have more space available, such as you would find in an average garage, then you can be more adventurous with your lighting schemes, introducing more sidelighting, for example, and toplighting, both of which require a free space around your subject.

Even if you don't like the formality of a studio setting, it is the place to learn most about how to control and create lighting effects, lessons that you can then apply to all of your photography – indoors and out.

▲ Floodlighting
For this profile of the sculptor Henry Moore the primary light source was a single floodlight, slightly above and face-on to him. From the camera's viewpoint, therefore, the lighting is from the side. This is a simple scheme you could emulate by using an add-on flashgun fitted with a diffuser.

◀ Spotlighting
Using the tightly controlled output from a spotlight produces a dramatic, localized effect, very different from the floodlit portrait above. Positioning your subject's face close to a desk lamp could give a similar effect. For a less controversial result, place a piece of white cardboard on the far side of the light to reflect a little illumination back into the subject's shadow side.

▶ Combined lighting
This portrait of writer Angus Wilson was taken with two diffused studio flash units placed at about 45° either side of him, and a small flash unit low down behind him to ensure that his distinguished silver hair was shown to advantage.

Available light

Although it is nearly always possible to introduce light from a flashgun, or some other artificial source, into a scene in order to increase the overall illumination, you then run the real risk of killing the very lighting effect that initially attracted you. In the overwhelming majority of cases, it's best to go with the light that is naturally present – the available light – be it daylight, domestic room lighting or even the flickering illumination from a candle. If you look for the right angle from which to shoot, and select the most

appropriate focal length, aperture and shutter speed, you should be able to overcome most lighting problems.

Colour temperature and contrast

One of the benefits of working in black and white is that you don't have to think about the colour temperature of the different light sources present in a scene. You can, for example, mix tungsten and daylight without producing the type of cast that occurs with colour film stock. The high ISO speeds

AVAILABLE LIGHT

◀ Window light
In this portrait of a thoughtful Henry Moore, the light from the window is extremely directional. To prevent one side of the sculptor's face disappearing completely into shadow, I used a white cardboard reflector on his shadow side. This gave a little detail on his cheek and reflected the merest glint of light in his otherwise shadowy eye.

▼ Silhouette lighting
One of the essential subject elements is shape, and here I emphasized this characteristic above all others by taking an exposure reading from the bright area of sky in the background. All it was then necessary to do was to get the model to adjust the angle of his head slightly so that you could see the outline of his beret, glasses and facial features clearly in the doorway.

available with black and white film also mean that you can opt to use an ISO 3200 emulsion, and carry on taking pictures with a handheld camera in the dingiest of lighting conditions.

However, even with the generous contrast-recording latitude of black and white, you may want to adjust the lighting effect by introducing a reflector to even out exposure differences between highlights and shadows when working with, say, window lighting. And if you intend to make your own prints (whether using an enlarger or a desktop computer set-up), you will in any event have a large measure of control over the density of specific parts of the image.

◀ Candlelight
Even with a high-ISO film, you will appreciate the large maximum aperture offered by standard lenses when taking shots like this. The contrast of the candlelighting is a positive asset when depth of field is shallow.

Landscapes

THE TOPIC OF landscape photography is very broad in concept and takes in far more than just rural settings. Most of us live in urban environments, for example – either in cities or large towns – and the only landscapes we are likely to be familiar with on a daily basis are ones largely covered with concrete and tarmac; but they are no less photographic for that. There are coastal landscapes, too, and here water may be the dominant natural feature. The fascinating aspect of all these landscapes is the way they constantly change, not only when seen at different times of day, but also from season to season, making them an inexhaustible resource for the observant photographer.

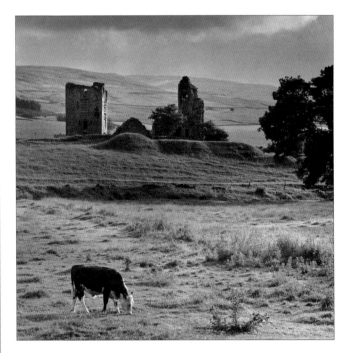

▲ Scale
Often in a landscape it is important to include something of known size, in order to impart a sense of scale to the scene. In this shot, the cow also helps to provide visual interest in what is otherwise a bland foreground.

◄ Tonal contrasts
It is the contrast in tone between the rich, deep blacks in the foreground and the much lighter-toned mist-shrouded background that lends depth and distance to this landscape view.

Foreground interest

LANDSCAPE PHOTOGRAPHS THAT hold your attention for more than just a perfunctory glance have usually been composed so that the pictorial elements they contain take your eye on a journey of discovery around the frame. Any image that reveals all it has to offer in the first few seconds will not sustain your interest for very long.

As the starting point for this journey, the foreground has an important role to play. First, you can use it as the hook with which to lead the

viewer in. Both of the images on the right illustrate this point, with the rocks in one and the sheep in the other acting as stepping stones, drawing you deeper and deeper into the composition. Second, the foreground can be used as a frame through which the rest of the image is viewed. The photograph below is an example of this. These types of effect are not difficult to pre-visualize if you use the camera's viewfinder as your principal compositional tool.

▶ Repeating shapes
Try to imagine how much less interesting this view of the Mont Saint Michel would be without the repeating shapes of the sheep taking your eye through the frame to rest on the distant abbey.

▼ Foreground frame
Two trees stand in the foreground, and the space between them seems to draw you deeper into the picture. This effect is accentuated by the strong tonal differences between foreground and background.

▲ Stepping stones
In order to bring the boulders to the very edge of the bottom of the frame it was necessary to crouch down low over the water. All the image planes are well separated here, with the telegraph poles defining a middle ground that separates the mountainous background from the rocky foreground

83

Stressing the vertical

I T IS SURPRISING how infrequently many photographers take advantage of the fact that practically all digital and film cameras have both vertical and horizontal framing options. Simply because the camera is more comfortable to use horizontally, this is how most pictures are taken – despite the requirements of the subject.

Vertically framed images tend to have a greater sense of movement and vitality than horizontally framed ones, and often they contain a better relationship between foreground and background picture elements. In a landscape scene, however, a vertical image may include a large area of sky, so make sure that this works to the picture's advantage before deciding on the framing.

In order to stress the vertical shape of your subject, experiment with different camera positions. A slightly low camera angle looking up at the subject, for example, will emphasize the vertical and any slight tapering or convergence of parallel lines that results may also work to your advantage.

One of the benefits using digital manipulation software (or an enlarger), is that even after you have taken the photograph, you can always crop it later to change a horizontally framed picture into a vertical one. You have more scope for reframing with a digital camera if you shoot at the highest resolution and quality settings available whenever possible – as you have more pixels that you can afford to sacrifice. If the subject matter warrants it, you can then crop a vertically framed shot even closer to produce a very long and thin print.

◀ **Cropping**
To emphasize the vertical nature of this composition, part of the negative was cropped during printing. The result is a powerful image, with the direction of the simple wooden grave marker echoing the upward thrust of the cathedral-like tree trunks behind.

▶ **Camera position**
Here, a slightly low camera position stresses the vertical thrust of the subject. Note how strongly, despite the disparity in their sizes, the visual link is made between the tree and small wooden hut.

Stressing the horizontal

I F YOU COMPARE the horizontally framed
pictures shown below and opposite with the
vertically-framed ones on the previous two pages
(*see pp. 84–5*), you will see an immediate difference
in the type and 'feel' of imagery they produce.

Horizontally framed pictures often tend to
give more of a sense of affinity between subject
elements adjacent to each other, and there is also
often a distinct sense of movement across the
frame. Strongly horizontal framing is nearly always
the first choice for panoramic-type photographs,
since this type of framing helps to capture the
feeling of spaciousness and atmosphere associated
with landscape scenes.

Even if you didn't notice the potential of a
scene when taking the picture, it is not too late to
change it afterwards. During printing or digital
editing you can crop the top and/or the bottom to
leave a horizontally framed image. Even if the
original uses the landscape format, cropping a
scenic shot to more panoramic proportions can
often create a more powerful picture.

▲ Partly obscured subject
The low-lying bank of mist partly obscuring the base of
the distant hills has helped to stress the horizontal nature
of this landscape composition. Seen like this, the tops of
the hills seem to be disconnected from the ground and
they look as if they are floating as a horizontal band across
the picture area.

▲ Sectional detail

Many scenes are capable of yielding a strongly horizontal image if you look for suitable details and then isolate them from their setting. This line of carved stonework figures is part of a tall, vertical structure but when framed with the camera held the other way around, the connections between these humorous-looking figures were not as strong or obvious.

▼ Darkroom cropping

To emphasize the patterns in this row of attractive wrought-iron balconies in Sydney, Australia, much of the top of the image was cropped off to produce a long, thin, panoramic image. Changing the shape of the image under the enlarger or using digital manipulation software can create a picture that is unusual, simply because it has a differently proportioned shape than usual.

Subdued light

THE VERY HIGH SPEEDS of film currently available make black and white an ideal medium when light levels are subdued. Whenever using a tripod is not possible, plan to match film speed to the prevailing conditions. If light levels are very low and you feel that your resulting negatives are lacking in contrast, then you could always experiment with different paper grades when printing (*see pp. 126–7*). For a normal-contrast negative, a grade 2 paper is often used; here, however, try printing on grade 4 or 5.

Early morning, before the sun has had a chance to warm the ground, is when you are most likely to encounter mist and fog. Although this type of lighting makes for wonderfully atmospheric images, you need to watch your exposure quite carefully, since exposure meters tend to read the scene as being brighter than it really is, leading to rather muddy prints lacking any clean, crisp, white tones. If in doubt, expose for the shadow areas.

If, when making your prints, you are not completely happy with the tonal balance, you can always hold back any parts of the image that are printing too dark or burn-in areas that are printing too light (*see p. 130*).

▲ Hard paper grade

One of the controls available to the black and white worker is the choice of paper grade. For this early-morning shot, a hard grade of paper was selected. The harder the paper, the less intermediate tones it reproduces (*see pp. 126–7*). Here you can see that the image is predominantly black and white, with few shades of grey. This effect can be recreated using Contrast, Levels and Curves controls found on digital manipulation programs.

◄ Soft paper grade

One of the effects of fog is to scatter the available light, producing a softly subdued type of lighting effect. No amount of burning-in would produce a satisfactory black, so it is best to use a soft paper grade (*see pp. 126–7*) and go for a more high-key type of result.

► Medium paper grade

Overhead foliage can greatly subdue even bright sunlight, as in this image. Here the negative showed a fully extended range of tones, which made it perfect for printing on a medium-grade paper (*see pp. 126–7*). The result is an image with good, dense blacks, clean whites and a wide range of greys in between.

Contrasty lighting

CONTRAST IS THE DIFFERENCE, assessed subjectively, between the brightest highlights and the deepest shadows contained in a scene. When this difference is extreme – such as at noon when the high, sun overhead creates intense highlights and casts correspondingly deep shadow, or at night when localized light sources from shop signs or car headlights brightly illuminate small areas while leaving most of the scene untouched – then the lighting is said to be contrasty.

While much advice is given to photographers on ways to avoid excessive contrast, many pictures, especially those in black and white, in fact benefit from the extra punch contrast can give. A high-contrast scene has to be approached carefully in terms of exposure, however. It is almost always best to set your exposure either for the highlights and let the shadows block up, or for the shadows and let the highlights burn out. A compromise exposure set somewhere between the two often results in a murky image of mid-tones, which lack any sparkle.

▼ Contrasty daylight
The rich blacks and strong whites of this scene are typical of the type of contrast produced by a bright sun overhead. You can exaggerate this effect further by printing on a hard grade of paper (*see pp. 126–7*).

▲ Contrast at night

The beams of light from the car's headlights, although powerful, cannot penetrate far into the oily darkness of night. Everything to the side of the light is therefore unaffected and remains near-black. The cat, caught in mid-stride, is backlit and side-on to the camera, and so appears as a perfect silhouette.

Adding drama

THE BLACK AND WHITE MEDIUM is purpose-made for adding a sense of drama to photographs. In normal vision, the landscape is full of colour: scores of different greens, the blues of the sky, coloured splashes of flowers and birds. Take all that away, and at once the world is simplified, becoming a gradation of tones from black to white, and thus giving the imagination the chance to invent its own colouring.

Film speed can be crucial, with the faster films producing a more obvious grain response that can add to the sense of foreboding in a dark, twilight landscape scene.

▼ The birds
This camera position, back inside a cave, makes it seem as if the photographer were in hiding, peering out tentatively at a garrulous gang of marauding gulls circulating with menace overhead.

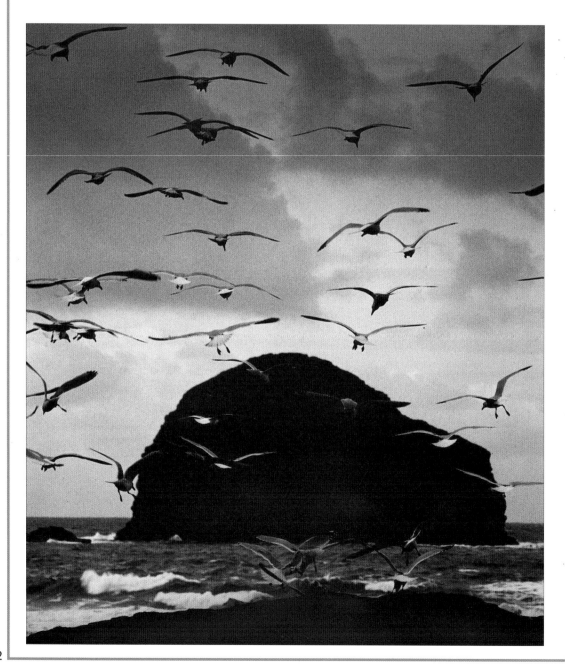

▶ Silhouetted view

A camera position halfway down the hillside was the best place to show this single stone cross against the only patch of brightness in an otherwise dark and stormy sky. In order to emphasize contrast, I took the exposure reading from the highlight and allowed the stark monument to show up as a silhouette. The grain of the fast, ISO 400 film used was accentuated a little by slightly extending the development time (*see pp. 120–21*).

▼ Storm light

A momentary break in the clouds allowed a broad beam of light through to illuminate the dark and bulky form of a castle perched high on a hillside. To increase the sense of drama, a bright highlight was added behind the castle's roof line, using a darkroom technique known as 'dodging' (*see p. 130*).

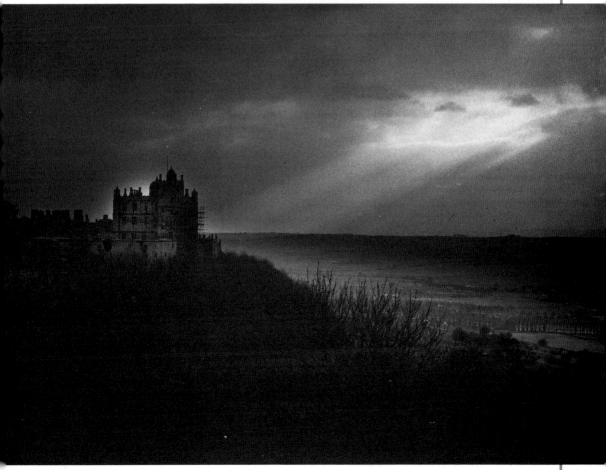

The idealized landscape

W E ALL HAVE, in our mind's eye, some personal notion of the idealized landscape – a place where man and nature come together in perfect harmony. The hard part, once you have found it, is to transform the colour scene before you into tones from black through grey to white while still capturing, or even enhancing, the spirit of the location.

Composition

Landscape shots most often need to be composed around some prominent feature. Pointing the camera in a random fashion is likely to result in disappointing pictures. Having determined the main focus of interest, experiment with different framings, adjusting focal length with the zoom and by trying out different viewpoints. Look carefully at how each change alters the visual relationship between your main subject and the other elements making up the shot.

As with all photographs taken with natural light, time of day is critical. Generally, the best light for landscapes occurs in the early morning and late afternoon. Light levels at these times may be lower than at noon, but the quality of the more directional illumination is superior. The overhead light of the noonday sun tends to destroy the illusion of form and depth, whereas the more oblique light of morning and afternoon strengthens these features.

◀ Dusk light

In this type of flat meadow landscape, finding a prominent feature around which to compose your picture can be difficult. To achieve it in this example, it was necessary to find just the right camera position and angle so that the foreground water reflected the rapidly dimming dusk light, creating a welcome highlight in an otherwise flat-toned scene. Of equal importance was showing the stepping stones leading across the waterlogged ground. These, in fact, are visually extremely important to the composition, acting as lead-in lines (*see pp. 28–9*) that take the viewer's eye across the water and into the landscape proper.

▲ Rustic harmony

This is the idealized rural scene for many people, with a broad river meandering through a tree-filled landscape. The only man-made intrusion is a rustic wooden fence, sensitively integrated, which has a stile to allow ramblers to cross unhindered. Here, too, the right camera position was crucial, for it is the fence and gate that bind this composition together and prevent the bright highlight on the water beyond becoming too prominent a feature in the scene. Angling the camera just slightly more in line with the river would also have brought more of the field on the left into view, and this was the least attractive aspect of the setting.

Romantic landscapes

THE IDEA OF THE ROMANTIC landscape means different things to different people. Each of us draws on our own background and experiences to bring together in our mind's eye the various elements that go to make up that special romantic setting.

Media input

Our notion of the romantic landscape must also be heavily influenced by the thousands of different images that are presented to us throughout our lives – the works of landscape painters seen in books, postcards and galleries, holiday posters in guidebooks and on billboards, and advertisements

on television. Your best approach is to look for a specific focal point around which to build your composition. This is always better than just snapping away. Analyse what it is about that scene that appeals to you, think what the key components of the scene are and then make sure that these features are also prominent in the way you frame the shot. It may be the way the light falls through the trees, creating areas of highlight and shadow, or it could be the pattern and texture of a carpet of fallen leaves.

Until you bring to the forefront of your mind what it is that attracts you to the scene, you will have trouble recording it on film or memory card.

◄ **The country cottage**
Glimpsed through overgrown shrubs and tall heads of flowers and grasses, a beam of sunlight lighting the way, the perfect country cottage – with vine-clad walls – nestles peacefully beneath the towering trees.

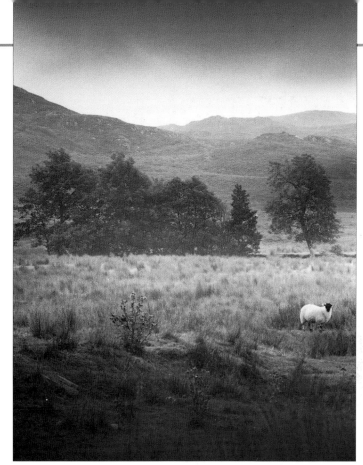

◄ Country idyll

With sunlight playing across the gentle hills, and a copse of trees helping to define the middle ground, you can almost hear the soft murmur of insects and the distant call of birdsong. To round off the scene, a sheep stands and stares contentedly back toward the camera, providing both a focal point and a sense of scale.

▼ Water

Water is one of the very most emotive of all the romantic devices. Here, the still surface of a placid river returns perfect reflections of the bankside trees and, invitingly in the foreground, a boat seems to beckon us into the frame.

Skyscapes

THE EVER-SHIFTING PATTERNS of clouds across the sky provide the landscape photographer with an unending source of inspiration. However, because black and white film reproduces blue as a light tone, often it is necessary to use a coloured filter to help restore or dramatize the tonal difference between the white clouds and blue sky (*see pp. 38–9*). Depending on how dramatic effect is required, try a yellow, an orange or a red filter. Slight underexposure will also help contrast. By pointing the camera directly upward you can exclude the land completely from the composition. Often, however, better pictures result from having at least a sliver of land at the bottom of the frame. An exposure taken from the sky, usually the brightest part of the scene, will probably leave the landscape underexposed, but the landscape is still important. It helps to define the picture area and it provides a scale against which the size of the sky can be judged.

▲ Scale

Only a ribbon of land remains, but the trees silhouetted against the bright sky toward the horizon, although fully grown and large, seem tiny compared with the enormity of the background of sky and cloud.

DIGITAL NOTES

• Digital editing on a PC allows you to tweak the contrast and exposure of a sky in ways that are not possible with traditional film techniques. Using gradient masks and adjustment layers, for instance, the sky and land can be manipulated in completely different ways, without the joins being visible. This allows far more control than burning-in a sky at a higher grade than the land using variable-contrast paper.

▶ Increasing contrast

The dramatic lighting in this cloud-dominated sky was enhanced by fitting an orange filter to the camera lens (*see pp. 38–9*). The sky now appears much darker in relation to the white clouds and the scene has really come to life.

▼ Using tone to effect

The ruggedness of this coastal scene has been mitigated by a soft-toned interpretation. By printing on soft-grade paper strong blacks and stark whites have been largely avoided.

Water views

INCLUDING WATER IN a photograph can give a new dimension to your composition. If the surface of the water is calm, and the angle of the light right, a body of water can turn into a perfect mirror-like reflector, repeating not only the shapes of the clouds above but also any features on the surrounding shoreline.

When the surface of the water is ruffled, other picture possibilities begin to emerge – abstract patterns of light and shade, for example, or star-like sparkles of intense highlight and zigzag reflections of familiar objects, which can make fascinating subjects for the camera in their own right.

Fast-flowing water is different yet again. Here you can use a fast shutter speed to freeze its movement or a slow speed to create a soft, impressionistic blur.

▼ Gentle ripples
Backlit and silhouetted, a small fishing boat and tender push through the calm water creating just sufficient disturbance to the surface to produce a slightly jagged, distorted set of reflections.

▲ Repeating images
Low evening light partially illuminates an old, stone-built boathouse, whose reflection is seen as a repeating image in the placid waters of the lake. The sense of depth is produced by the significantly lighter tones of the distant hills. This is known as aerial perspective.

▶ Choosing a shutter speed
A shutter speed of 1/15 sec was used to photograph this rapidly flowing stream. For maximum impact, the soft blurring and streaking of the water has to be contrasted with the pin-sharp clarity of the surrounding rocks. To achieve this, use the smallest aperture your lens has to offer and mount the camera on a sturdy tripod. If the light is bright, you may have to use a neutral density (ND) filter to obtain a slow enough shutter speed without the risk of overexposure.

◀ Choosing an exposure
With a backlit scene you have to decide whether to set exposure for the shadows and let the highlights burn out, or to expose for the bright areas of the frame and let the shadows fill in, as in this example.

Reflections

THE PRESENCE OF A BODY OF WATER often adds another dimension to a photograph. The surface of still water can introduce a certain 'confusion' to a picture, becoming a mirror-like surface reflecting an image of the surrounding shoreline features or sky so perfect that it is difficult to tell which is real. Moving water, or that disturbed by a pebble or stone, is entirely different, with the reflected image distorted in all manner of unpredictable ways. Sometimes the image will still be recognizable as a reflection of the original; sometimes it will be a wildly chaotic and abstract pattern of tones. You do not need a large amount of water to add reflections to a photograph. Next time it rains, notice how even quite small puddles of water in the roadway or gutter can reflect back images of the surrounding buildings, trees or sky. However, you will have to search to find the best angle so that the reflections add strength and excitement to the picture, and show just that part of the scene you wish to record.

▲ Disturbed water
Composing the image with the water at the bottom of the frame has added real interest to the foreground. The arrangement of garden furniture at the top has a graphic simplicity, while the distorted reflections give a very different interpretation of the same scene.

▶ Calm water
The strong lines of the bridge and lamp in this shot help to define and contain the rest of the image, which is shrouded in morning mist. In the calm water below, however, the mirror-like reflection shows a stronger, more contrasty and detailed view of the riverside scene.

People in a landscape

T HE THREE PHOTOGRAPHS on these pages depict very different types of landscape – a beach scene; a vast, largely featureless plain in the heartland of Romania; and a misty English orchard in winter – but each has been brought to life by the inclusion of the human figure.

There is virtually no landscape left on the planet where the hand of man is not somehow in evidence, so the inclusion of people in the frame can lend a certain authenticity to your pictures.

More importantly, however, the human figure is of known size, and so the scale of the landscape in which it is portrayed can easily be gauged by comparing one with the other. The figure does not need to be the principal subject of the shot to fulfil this function, nor does it even have to be particularly prominent. If stuck for suitable passers-by, you could use a tripod or some other type of support, with your camera's self-timer, to include yourself in the picture.

▲ The importance of scale
Without the inclusion of this boy and his donkey in the shot, it would be impossible to gauge either the size of the foreground tree or the extent of the landscape it overlooks.

▶ Humorous content
The gloominess generated by the damp, clinging fog lying low over the ground of this wintry orchard scene is relieved by the humorous inclusion of the back view of a man carrying a piece of garden statuary.

◀ Exposing for effect
The inclusion of bathers is vital for the success of this beach scene. About 2½ stops of 'overexposure' was necessary to burn out the detail of the water and sand, so as to create an almost high-key scene. This leaves the figures slightly reduced in prominence as the intensity of the light eats into their form.

Urban landscapes

THE URBAN LANDSCAPE is perhaps not generally thought of as visually exciting, but it is undeniably so. While you can't liken the towering buildings of a city centre to a forest of trees, or compare the ribbons of tarmac roadways with the meandering channels of rivers, the photographic approach can be surprisingly similar.

Unless your intention is to accentuate such features as pattern, repeating shape or texture, the need for a strong composition often means finding a principal focus of attention. Lighting direction is also vital, with morning and afternoon sunlight often providing the most striking contrasts. And scale is just as important in an urban setting as in a rural one, to add a sense of drama and a way of gauging the extent of the scene.

And at night, when the streets are full of lights from houses, cars, stores and signs, you can use a solid tripod to carry on shooting through until the following morning.

▲ Repeating shapes
An electricity pylon might not seem to be the most promising of subjects. But shot from below its metal skeleton, it is turned into a mosaic of dark lines that create a pattern against the lighter tone of the overcast sky.

◀ Power play
Looking incongruous in a predominantly rural setting, these four massive power station cooling towers loom ominously above the foreground field. The bare winter branches of the tree, in the immediate foreground help to mask off much of the field to the left of the picture, so concentrating the viewer's attention on the pony grazing unconcerned and the children playing on the swings as the pollution drifts overhead.

▲ Telephoto compression
This industrial urban scene was shot with a long telephoto zoom setting, with a focal length of around 250mm. Its very narrow angle of view has excluded much distracting detail between my camera position and the female subject, and I was far enough away for her not to take any notice. One of the effects of a long lens like this is to compress the apparent distance between objects. This has made the houses appear to be built closer together and has also enlarged the background in relation to the foreground, making the pit machinery seem oppressively large and close.

Architecture

THE SUBJECT OF architectural photography is broad. As you can see from the pictures on these pages and those that follow, buildings embrace everything from grand country houses to cathedrals, humble corner shops to ruined shells, architectural details and the less familiar building styles of far-off places.

Time of day

The direction of light striking the subject is critical, and this is dependent on the time of day and the sun's position in the sky. Frontal and toplighting has the effect of flattening contrast, assigning similar tonal values to all parts of the building, and thus decreasing the sense of depth. Sidelighting, however, will strike some parts of a building while throwing others into shadow. The contrast between lit and unlit surfaces exaggerates the texture of the building's façade and often creates a more interesting interpretation.

Rather than take a picture from the angle you first come across, take the time to walk around the subject. If the light is not perfect on one face of the building, it may well be just what you are looking for at the side or rear. This way, you may also avoid including people in the shot.

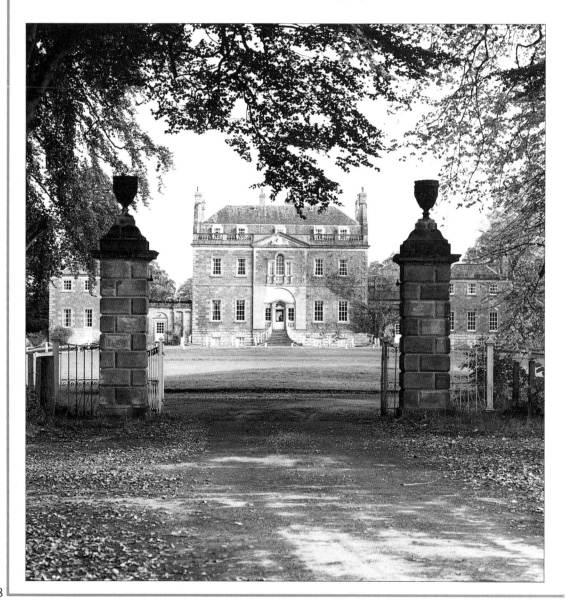

DIGITAL NOTES

• Programs like Photoshop allow you to correct the converging verticals created by pointing wide-angle lenses upwards at tall buildings. They let you stretch the top of the structure and shrink the base, creating an effect similar to that achieved with a shift lens.

▶ Wide-angle distortion

Typical of of Thailand and Cambodia, this shrine, or *chedi*, has been photographed with a wide-angle lens used close to the base of the structure. With the lens pointing upward, note how the building's already tapering top has been exaggerated, producing a much steepened perspective.

◀ Framing

To mask an area of toneless sky, the camera angle was selected to show the house framed by overhanging foliage.

▲ Time of day

A low sun throws shadows across the lawn, striking only the prominent features of the building. The shadows created give a strongly three-dimensional result.

▲ Lenses to isolate

A standard zoom lens was used to take this shot of what has almost become a historical footnote – the local corner shop.

Choice of lens and camera position

The most generally useful lens for architectural photography that non-specialists are likely to own is probably a zoom, one with a focal length range of about 28–100mm (for 35mm cameras). The wide-angle end of this range will allow you to include all of even quite large buildings from reasonably close up. A wider zoom range, such as that offered by a 17–35mm lens, will prove particularly useful for interiors, but will also help give variation to exterior shots.

Moving in with a wide-angle and pointing the camera up to include the tops of buildings produces an effect called converging verticals, which, although dramatic, makes structures appear to topple backwards. A special shift lens will prevent this happening because the lens can be shifted off-centre while the camera, and film, stay parallel with the subject. However, not only are these expensive, they are only available for some SLRs.

▲ Architectural detail
Sometimes you want to record only a small detail of a building, such as in the example here. To restrict my angle of view and get the subject large in the frame, I needed to use a telephoto lens setting.

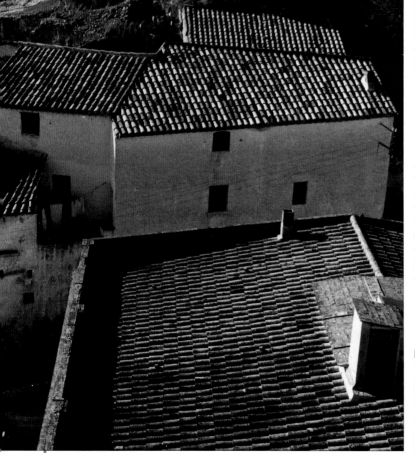

◀ Repeating pattern
The best angles for photography can often be the most unlikely ones. In this overhead view, the buildings' most attractive features – their symmetrically tiled roofs – are emphasized as a repeating pattern of light and shade created by the raking light of a low sun.

▶ Unlikely candidate
The interior of this building was gutted centuries ago, and what the low camera position has now recorded is the bare bones of the architecture – soaring pillars and massively heavy stone walls pierced by elegant window arches.

Interiors

UNLESS YOU CAN BRING a lot of artificial light to bear, you will usually be heavily dependent on daylight entering through windows or doors when photographing interiors.

In a large interior, window light may result in large areas of impenetrable shadow in the farther reaches of the space so, rather than include the whole interior, concentrate on well-lit details instead.

In a small-scale interior, problems are usually fewer and easier to solve. Even if window light does result in dark areas, these can often be relieved with a small flashgun or a reflector or two. Using black and white film means that you can turn on the ordinary domestic room lights to boost the overall level of illumination without worrying about the colour casts that mixed lighting creates.

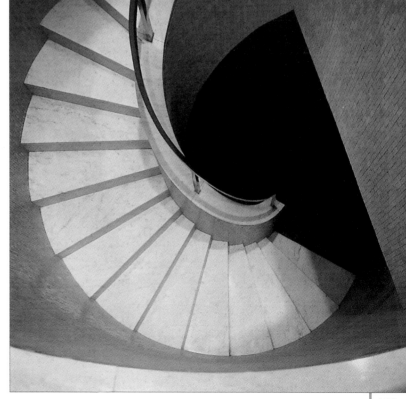

▲ Small-scale interior
Light from the window and the ceiling lamp have created areas of brightness that cut across an otherwise dark sitting room. The resulting mix of light and shade creates a dramatic portrait of the woman sitting in her own home.

▶ Interior detail
This small section of the stairwell of a modern building presented the best opportunity for a uniformly lit image. The selective view from overhead has also created an interestingly abstract set of flowing geometric lines and shapes.

◀ Large-scale interior
Luckily, the interior of this church building was well endowed with windows. This made the lighting generally even, but still a tripod was essential to hold the camera steady during a 1½ sec exposure at f16. The striated lighting effect is caused by beams of sunlight scattering in the dusty atmosphere.

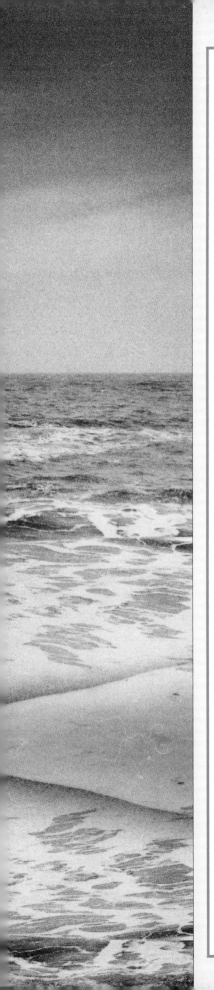

The traditional darkroom

IN YEARS GONE BY, photographers began by taking black and white pictures and only when they were proficient in that medium did they move on to colour. In those days, a darkroom was a major part of the photographer's equipment, whether amateur or professional.

Today, it is different. Photographers begin with colour and, right at the start, nearly all either use highly automated photographic laboratories to develop and print their work, or create their hard copies from their computer desktop.

Black and white film photography has now turned into something of a traditional craft only practised by a hard core of enthusiasts. Those that try black and white film occasionally might try to get their work developed and printed commercially. The results are, more often than not, disappointing. Commercial laboratories are not set up for black and white processing the way they are for colour and, unless you pay top prices for top professional printers, you will never get the type of quality you hoped for. Nor will you have the creative control over your film developing and print-making that is so much a part of good black and white photography.

The answer is to set up your own darkroom at home. For the black and white worker, this is neither as difficult nor as expensive as you might imagine. And you will be surprised at how quickly you start to learn the basics of the print-maker's craft.

◀ **Darkroom control**
A multiple print such as this (*see p. 131*) creates an intriguing composition. Only with your own darkroom, however, can you have full control over the look of the final print.

Setting up a darkroom

THE PRIME NEED for a darkroom is a contained area that can be blacked out. This is not that difficult, especially if you have an internal room or a closet without windows. If there is a window, cover it with a light-proof shutter or buy blackout blinds from a specialist camera store. Don't forget to check the door area. A lot of light can find its way under and around a door and its hinges. Commercially available draught excluders can be used to help here.

Another important requisite is electricity. This is not likely to be a problem if you are using a normal room in the house, but if you are converting a bathroom or understairs cupboard, use a professional electrician to take care of any installation.

You will need facilities for two lights – a normal white (room) light and a special darkroom safelight. Each will need its own draw cord switch to guard against touching electrical switches with wet hands. You will also need an electrical socket for the enlarger and at least one other for a timer or dish warmers.

Running water is a big advantage in any darkroom, but it is by no means a necessity. Providing you have access to running water nearby, much darkroom work can be carried out with just a bucket of fresh water.

In any darkroom, divide the space between the dry side – the enlarger, negatives, printing papers and switches – and the wet side – chemicals, processing dishes and water supply – in order to avoid accidents.

▲ Understairs darkroom

An understairs cupboard can make a suitable darkroom, with the advantage of there not being a window to worry about. Plan the available space carefully. Because of the sloping stairs above, one end of the room will be higher than the other, so start by positioning the enlarger where the head can travel to the top of its column. Build in benches at a comfortable working height and position processing dishes as far away from the enlarger as possible. Include storage cupboards and space for a water bucket.

To black out a bathroom, fit a light-proof blind that can be rolled up when the darkroom is not in use. You can buy blinds set in a frame with Velcro along the sides to improve the light seal.

Place a board across the bath to make a working surface and wash prints in the bathroom sink.

Bathrooms do not have conventional electrical sockets, so you will need an extension cable with a distribution box.

▲ Bathroom darkroom

A temporary darkroom such as this can be set up in a few minutes and packed away out of sight just as quickly.

▲ Permanent darkroom

If you have the space for a permanent darkroom, black out the window and door, have running water laid on and adjust the position of electrical sockets to bench height. Paint the room white to reflect the safelight, but paint the area around the enlarger itself matt black. Organize two distinct areas: a dry bench for the enlarger and a wet bench for the processing dishes. A light-tight extractor fan is useful to keep the air circulating – important in a room with no window and in which chemical fumes can sometimes prove unpleasant and unhealthy.

Equipping the darkroom

EQUIPPING A HOME DARKROOM is not as expensive as you might initially think. Black and white darkroom work is divided into two areas: developing and printing. Developing is when you take the film from your camera and process it in standard chemicals to produce a strip of negatives. Printing involves taking those negatives and, using an enlarger, producing a set of prints from them. The processing stages for film and print developing are very similar.

You can get started with only the most basic equipment. It can be bought from a good photographic dealer, but secondhand darkroom equipment, and even complete darkrooms, are often seen for sale at reasonable prices in the classified advertisements found at the back of popular photographic magazines, at garage sales, or on online auction sites such as eBay.

▲ Time, temperature and lighting

A darkroom clock is better than using your watch for timing. It has a large face that is easy to read and counts off minutes and seconds in ascending or descending order. Printing paper is insensitive to the colour produced by a darkroom safelight, so black and white printing can be carried out in its light. The thermometer is used for checking the temperature of chemicals used in processing. In black and white, only the developer temperature is critical.

▲ Basic equipment

The developing tank (*right*) is a light-tight container with a light trap in its lid. Chemicals can be poured in and out, but light is prevented from entering. Inside the tank, the film is held on a plastic spiral.

Two basic chemicals are needed for developing and printing: developer and fixer. A stop bath is also useful, but it can be replaced by plain water. The same fixer can be used, at different dilutions, for developing film and for making prints. Although some 'universal' developers can also be used for both processes, it is advisable to use different types of developer for processing film and paper.

The dishes are used only for printing. Since the process can be carried out by safelight, there is no need for light-tight equipment at this stage.

The graduated cylinder is used for measuring the dilution of the chemicals, and the tongs are useful for lifting prints in and out of the processing trays.

EQUIPPING THE DARKROOM

The enlarger is rather like a projector, only one that projects its image vertically on to a baseboard, rather than horizontally on to a wall or screen. It is used to project and size the negative on the sensitive printing paper.

You can alter the size of the print, or crop it for the best composition, by adjusting the height of the enlarger head above the baseboard. Sharpness is defined by the enlarger's focusing control. The enlarger lens has f stops, just like a camera lens. Stopping the lens down reduces the brightness of the image and, just as small apertures increase depth of field in a camera lens, so this also helps to ensure accurate focus on the baseboard. Always focus at maximum aperture, however, to take advantage of the brightest possible image.

The printing, or enlarging, easel on the baseboard holds the paper flat. By moving its adjustable arms, you can decide on the shape of print you want by masking off the edges of the paper to leave white borders. Standing on the baseboard is a magnifier, used for checking focus of the negative.

Beside the enlarger is a timer, which is used to time the exposure of the paper. Just as with a camera, stopping the lens down requires longer exposures, but instead of the fractions of a second usual for film, paper requires many seconds of exposure time. If linked electrically to the enlarger, the timer automatically turns the light off when the appropriate time has elapsed.

When setting up the enlarger, make sure that it is positioned on a solid, flat surface that is not prone to vibrations. The slightest movement of the enlarger during printing will spoil the print.

▼ Choosing an enlarger

The enlarger is the most expensive piece of equipment you will have to buy when equipping a darkroom. It is also the most important, so buy the best you can afford. Make sure that the enlarger is sturdy and does not wobble easily. Check that the movement of the head up and down on its column is smooth and easy to control. Enlargers are sold with a choice of lenses, so always buy the best quality you can. There is no point taking pictures with an expensive camera lens and then printing them through an inferior enlarger lens.

Processing silver-based film

WITH THE DARKROOM EQUIPPED, you are ready to begin processing a film. For this stage you only need a developing tank and a spiral. You must remove the film from its cassette and load it into the tank in total darkness, but once the lid is in place, all other steps can be carried out in normal room lighting. If you use a changing bag (a light-tight cloth bag with elasticated openings to insert your hands) you don't even need a darkroom at all for this stage.

◀ Tank types
The developing tank uses a spiral to hold the coils of film apart. Different sizes can be used depending on whether 35mm or 120 rollfilm is being developed. Some tanks take two spirals so that two films can be processed at the same time.

1 Ensure the spiral is clean and bone dry before you start. In darkness, remove the film from its cassette, cut off the shaped leader and feed the end into the opening of the spiral.

2 Hold one side of the spiral and rotate the other until you feel it stop. Turn the first side back and repeat the process. By this means, the whole film is fed into the spiral.

3 If the film jams, gently unwind it a little and try again. Never force the process. When the whole film is in the spiral, use scissors to cut it away from the cassette spool.

4 Place the loaded spiral into the tank and spin it to make sure that there are no obstructions. Replace the lid of the tank. The ordinary room light can now be turned on.

Chromogenic film

This film is processed in C-41 colour chemistry, and many photographers have it developed commercially. The chemicals are available in kit form, however, and the resulting negatives are printed just like conventional black and white films.

▲ Professional temperature control
When processing chromogenic film, the temperature of the chemicals is critical. One way of keeping the temperature constant is to buy a processing unit with a thermostatically controlled water bath surrounding the chemicals. A motor turns the developing tank to ensure even processing.

◀ Informal temperature control
If you do not have a professional processing unit like the one above, stand the chemicals and film-processing tank in a bowl of water that has been preheated to the correct temperature. Add more warm water from a kettle as the temperature in the bowl drops below that recommended.

PROCESSING SILVER-BASED FILM

With silver-based black and white film, only the temperature of the developer is critical if you want to hold to the recommended timings. While the temperatures of other solutions should not vary by wide amounts, these do not affect the timing or the effectiveness of the chemistry in the same way as they do with the developer. If the temperature of the developer differs from that recommended you will need to adjust the length of this processing stage. Details of timings, for a range of temperatures, are given in the developer's instruction sheet. Development time also varies with the ISO speed the film has been used at. Take the time to familiarize yourself with these instructions.

5 Dilute the chemicals according to the instruction sheet. Once diluted, check the temperature – 68°F (20°C) is usually recommended.

6 As you pour the developer into the tank, start the timer. Pour in a steady flow, then gently rap the tank to dislodge air any bubbles.

7 Rotate the spirals for 10 seconds in every minute during development, or invert the tank, to bring fresh developer into contact with the film.

8 When development time is up, pour the developer away. The best developers are 'one-shot' solutions – used once and then discarded.

9 Reset the timer to zero and pour in the diluted stop bath. This stage can be replaced by two or three washes in water (ensure it is not too cold).

10 If stop bath is used, pour it out of the tank after the time recommended in its instruction sheet. This solution can be kept for reuse.

11 Reset the timer to zero and pour in diluted fixer. Agitate the spiral regularly throughout the time recommended in its instructions.

12 Pour out the fixer and keep it for future films. Wash the film in gently running water, and after about 30 minutes hang it up to dry.

13 Use squeegee tongs to remove excess water droplets, and then leave the film in a dust-free area until it has completely dried.

Assessing the negative

A CORRECTLY EXPOSED, correctly developed negative should have a full range of tones from nearly clear to almost solid black. As a general rule of thumb, place a negative on a sheet of newspaper. If it has been correctly exposed and developed,

you should just about be able to read the print through the darkest areas. Underdevelopment produces a low-contrast negative with a thin image in which highlights and shadow areas vary very little in intensity. Overdevelopment, however, leads

Correct exposure, correct development

▲ The negative shows a full range of tones throughout the image. The numbers in the film's rebate are dark, crisp and clear.

Correct exposure, under-development

▲ The negative is thin and lacks contrast, although there is still detail in the shadow areas. The numbers in the film's rebate are too light.

Underexposure, correct development

▲ The negative is generally too thin and the shadow areas are badly defined. The numbers in the film's rebate are crisp and clear.

Underexposure, under-development

▲ The negative is far too thin and it lacks any contrast. The numbers in the film's rebate are too light.

Overexposure, correct development

▲ The negative is generally too dense. The shadow areas are blocking up, or merging. The numbers in the film's rebate are crisp and clear.

Overexposure, under-development

▲ The negative looks correct at first sight, but detail is not as sharply defined as it should be. The numbers in the film's rebate are too light.

to a dense negative, in which the image appears to be very contrasty.

Under- and overdevelopment can be confused with under- and overexposure, but there is a difference. Shadow areas (the light areas of the negative) will be clear if the image has been underexposed, but will still register if the exposure was correct, even if the negative was underdeveloped. Overexposure gives a coarse-grained negative.

Correct exposure, overdevelopment

▲ The negative is too dark and contrasty overall. The numbers in the film's rebate are also too dark and they are tending to spread out and fatten up.

Underexposure, overdevelopment

▲ The negative looks correct at first sight, but shadow areas are lacking detail. The numbers in the film's rebate are too dark and tending to spread out.

Overexposure, overdevelopment.

▲ The negative is far too dense and contrasty. The numbers in the film's rebate are also too dark and they are tending to spread out.

Processing faults

The worst fault is when there is no image at all. Completely clear film means that it has not been exposed. If there are no edge numbers either, it has not been developed. Totally black film means that it has been exposed to light, in the camera or darkroom.

◀ Fogged film, due to light getting into the cassette. The resulting streaks of light have developed as dark areas on the negative.

◀ The streaks on this negative are sections of the film that have been exposed but not developed. This is caused by not having sufficient developer in the developing tank.

◀ The lines on this negative are stress marks. They have been caused by the film kinking as it was forced into the developing tank spiral.

◀ The marks on this negative are due to the emulsion beginning to break up. This can occur if there is a huge difference in the temperatures of the different solutions.

Making a print

THE PROCESS OF MAKING a black and white print is dependent on working from a reverse-toned negative. This is because areas of the film emulsion struck by light, after development, darken in proportion to the strength of the original illumination. This is why negatives are dark where the original subject was light, and vice versa.

When making a print, a negative is projected on to a piece of sensitive paper and the image is formed in the same way as when a camera lens projects an image on to film. Here, however, the dark areas of the negative inhibit the transmission of the light, and so shield those parts of the paper. When developed, these areas are therefore light in tone. What you are actually making is a negative of a negative – a positive.

Unlike film, black and white printing paper is insensitive to red or orange light. This allows you to use a safelight of one of these colours, as long as it is not positioned too close to the enlarger or the processing dishes.

Before making a print, you should first make a test strip (*see below*) to assess the correct exposure that will be needed under the enlarger.

Focusing the enlarger

1 Clean the negative with a blower brush or compressed air. Put it into the enlarger's negative carrier and then push this into the enlarger. The negative should be shiny-side up, but with the image upside down.

2 Turn the room light off and the enlarger on. Adjust the height of the head to produce the required size of image on the easel. Adjust the focusing control. Use a focus magnifier to check.

3 Focus at the enlarger lens's widest aperture, but then close down two or three stops before making the exposure. This will give greater depth of field and so help correct any focusing inaccuracy.

Exposing the test strip

1 Turn off the enlarger and, with the safelight on, take a sheet of paper out of its sealed bag and place it in the easel, shiny side up. Turn the timer and enlarger on at the same time to begin exposing.

2 After 2 seconds, cover a small strip of the paper, using a piece of opaque card. After another 2 seconds, cover another strip of the paper and continue in the same way every 2 seconds.

3 Continue until you have covered the whole sheet of paper. This means that you have now exposed successive strips of the paper for 2 seconds, 4 seconds, 6 seconds, 8 seconds, and so on.

Processing the test strip

The next stage is processing the test strip, which is carried out in dishes by the light of the safelight. The chemistry for this is much the same as that used for film – developer, stop bath (or wash) and fix. The stop bath and fixer used for film development can also be used here, although different dilutions are usually recommended. It is best, however, to use a developer formulated specifically for prints. This can be kept for short periods and reused for later printing sessions.

1 Slide the paper quickly and evenly under the surface of the developer, ensuring that the whole area is covered.

2 Throughout development, gently rock the dish. The image will soon appear on the paper and strengthen rapidly.

3 After the recommended time, remove the print from the developer, using the print tongs to protect your fingers.

4 Allow excess developer to drain into the dish, then slip the print into the stop bath or water dish for the recommended time.

5 Drain the print and place it into the fixer for the recommended time. After one minute, you can turn on the room light.

6 Wash the print in running water, or place it in a dish or bucket of water and transfer to running water as soon as possible.

◄ **The test strip**
You have now exposed and printed your test strip. There is no need to dry it in order to assess it, but you should make the assessment in white light or daylight. The test strip will show the image with different bands of density, each corresponding to the length of time it was exposed under the enlarger light.

▶ **The finished print**
Choose the strip that exhibits the best range of tones and expose the complete print for this amount of time. Process the final print in exactly the same way as you did the test strip.

Choice of paper

PRINTING PAPER is not all the same. Black and white paper is available in different contrast grades and with different surface finishes designed to give a range of different effects.

The two most widely used surfaces are glossy and matt. When you begin, you will probably use glossy, because this produces a richer black and a sharper-looking image than matt-finish types.

Most printing papers today are resin-coated. These papers have a special finish that prevents liquid soaking into the paper base, and so are quicker and easier to process. Traditional papers are fibre based. These give a richer range of tones, but they take longer to process, wash and dry.

Paper grades are designated by numbers, usually 0–6. Grade 2 is normal. Lower numbers are 'softer', meaning that the image will be less contrasty and contain an extended range of mid-tones. Higher numbers are 'harder', making them more contrasty since some or, depending on the grade, many of the mid-tones are omitted.

'Variable contrast' or 'multi-grade' papers are capable of giving a range of different contrasts on the same sheet of paper, depending on the way the enlarger light is filtered. Magenta light makes the paper harder, while yellow light makes the same paper softer and less contrasty.

◀ A correctly exposed and correctly developed negative. The same negative was used to make all three of the prints shown on this page.

▲ Printed on a soft grade of paper, the correctly exposed and developed negative produces a low-contrast print.

▲ With a medium or normal grade of paper, the print exhibits a full range of tones from black to just a little lighter than the base of the paper.

▲ On a hard grade of paper, the same negative produces a high-contrast print with a restricted range of grey tones between black and white.

CHOICE OF PAPER

VC PAPER

• Variable contrast (VC) paper allows printers to get different printing grades without the need to purchase several types of paper.

• More significantly, different grades can be combined in one print. The sky of a landscape, for instance, can be burnt-in at a grade 5 to give a dramatic contrasty effect, whilst the rest of the image can be exposed at at normal contrast (grade 2).

◀ **Contact sheet**
To decide which negatives to print, and how, make a contact sheet by placing strips of negatives, emulsion-side down, in contact with a sheet of printing paper. Place a sheet of clean glass on top to hold the negatives flat and expose them under the enlarger. Make a test strip to determine exposure and then process the paper as normal (*see pp. 124–5*). Comparing negatives like this will also help to show you which grades of paper might be best for each particular picture.

A high-contrast negative (*above*) could produce a fairly normal print on a soft grade of paper. Alternatively, it can be printed on a hard grade to produce a more striking, high-contrast print (*left*).

A low-contrast negative (*above*), printed on a soft grade of paper, reduces the range of intermediate tones in the final print and leads to this pleasing low-contrast type of result (*left*).

Composing on the baseboard

PHOTOGRAPHERS WHO USE commercial processing laboratories, instead of doing their own developing and printing, miss out on all the creativity of darkroom work.

In the darkroom, the composition of the original image on the negative can be subtly changed, depending on how the picture is cropped or which portion of the negative is chosen for enlargement. In many cases, the same negative can produce two or three very different prints – each good in its own terms – depending on how it is handled at the printing stage.

In this regard, darkroom processing and printing can be every bit as original and creative as the initial photography. Such cropping techniques are also easily accessible using a digital darkroom.

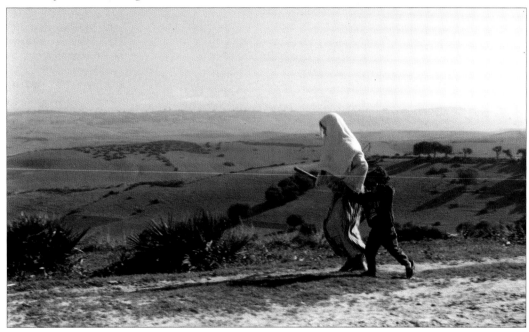

▲ Traditional crop
Here, a negative has been cropped with the emphasis on traditional picture composition, placing the figures on the right of the frame and thus leaving space on the left for them to move into.

◀ Creating emphasis
Here, the same negative has been recomposed on the enlarger base-board to give additional emphasis to the figures themselves. This has been achieved by removing much of the surrounding landscape.

▲ Vertical cropping

Not every subject fits comfortably into the traditional format of a camera's viewfinder. Tall subjects can be cropped and the prints trimmed to make a much narrower picture than normal, thus emphasizing the shape of the subject.

▲ Removing clutter

You can often improve the composition of a picture simply by selecting the best area for enlargement. In the original picture (*top*) too much extraneous detail has been included. The man at the café table is lost in a distracting background and the eye wanders all over the frame, taking too much notice of unimportant aspects. In the second picture (*above*) the picture has been cropped and enlarged to give emphasis to the man, who is the principal subject of the picture.

▼ Horizontal cropping

In the same way as that demonstrated in the example above, subjects that demand more of a horizontal, panoramic format can be easily cropped under the enlarger to make a longer panoramic-style picture, one with less height than usual.

Shading and burning-in

UNTIL NOW, the assumption has been that the test strip (*see pp. 124–5*) helps to determine the best exposure time for the whole print. In fact, with many pictures it is a good idea to give different parts of the paper very different exposures.

The test strip, for example, might indicate that the sky reproduces better with less exposure than the ground, whereas a bright white wall of a building needs more exposure than its surrounding landscape in order to retain detail in the brickwork. That's the time to start shading and burning-in.

▲ Tools of the trade
Shading (or dodging) and burning-in are ways of controlling the tone of a print. By holding a piece of card over some of the paper for part of the exposure, you lighten the tone of that area. To burn-in, cover all of the paper part-way through, except for the part you want darker.

▲ Techniques
Some printers use their hands, others pieces of card, to make shadows over the paper to locally reduce exposure times.

No matter which technique you use, keep the shader constantly moving to prevent abrupt differences in tone appearing.

◀ Before and after
These two pictures show the differences you can achieve by reducing or increasing the density of local areas of a print. All of the first print (*top left*) was printed at a single exposure and there is a great range of tonal response throughout the image. The larger print (*left*) has had very different treatment. The bottom of the print received the same exposure as the first. It was then shaded with a piece of cardboard while the rest of the image received 50 per cent additional exposure to burn-extra detail into what were formerly rather bleached and empty parts of the picture. If multi-grade paper is used, such areas can also be burnt-in using a different grade (*see page 127*).

Multiple printing

MULTIPLE PRINTING involves printing parts of two or more negatives on the same sheet of paper. The technique can be used for something as simple as adding a sky from one negative to a landscape from another. It can also be more extreme, with several negatives being used to build up a composite and surreal final print.

If the area into which you want to add a second image is dark on the first negative, therefore printing light in the final picture, you can simply expose two negatives in succession on the same sheet of paper. If, however, the combination involves more complicated images, you will need to mask certain areas of the first print in order to leave space for the appropriate part of the second image to be printed into.

First, size up the various negatives to be used on a plain sheet of paper, sketching in the way each is going to fall in the finished picture. Next, make test strips for each negative to determine the different exposure times needed. Then use the master sketch to make the masks that you will use to block certain parts of each picture during each of the exposures, much like the shading and burning-in techniques (*see opposite*).

▲ First original
With this sized up, a mask was cut from the middle of a piece of card to the shape of the hole.

▲ Second original
The scene into which the face is to be inserted. This was exposed with the circular mask held over the central part of the sky.

▲ The final result
The shape left when cutting the original mask was used to cover all but the shape of the hole, through which the first negative was printed.

Sandwich printing

SANDWICH PRINTING is similar to, and sometimes confused with, multiple printing (*see p. 131*), although they are different techniques producing different results. To make a sandwich print, two negatives are placed together in the enlarger's negative carrier and the resulting combination is then printed as normal. It is a straightforward technique, but the original negatives need to be chosen with great care.

To work best, one negative should have sharply delineated areas of light and dark, so that the image of the second negative can record through the clear areas of the first. It is best if one of the images is of some recognizable subject, such as a landscape or a portrait, while the other, which will overlay the first with its texture, is more abstract.

Often it is a good idea to shoot the secondary images specifically for the purpose. Any textured surface tends to work well: bricks, stonework, basketweave, even a dense pattern of tree branches against a clear sky.

Because the sandwich of two negatives is necessarily dense, it helps if the initial images are a little underdeveloped to make them thinner than usual. It also helps to place the negatives emulsion to emulsion (non-shiny-sides together), so that the actual images are more in the same plane and therefore easier to focus together.

◄ Texture overlay
To make this sandwich print, two negatives were combined in the enlarger's negative carrier. The first was a standard studio portrait; the second was a close-up of the woven pattern on a straw basket. The two slightly underdeveloped negatives were placed in contact and then exposed and processed in the normal way.

Using lith film

WHEN PROCESSED CORRECTLY, lith film gives a 'soot and whitewash' effect, recording only dense black and pure white and eliminating all the intermediate tones of grey. To achieve this stark, contrasty effect, it is best to process the film in a special lith developer. Failing that, process it in print, rather than film, developer.

Lith film is used to make intermediate negatives or internegs for various specialist darkroom effects and exposures.

Lith film is most commonly sold in sheet form. It is exposed like a print under an enlarger, from a 35mm negative, then contact printed to provide a final print. It is orthochromatic, which means that it is insensitive to red light, and so can be used in the light of a red darkroom safelight.

▲ **Normal result**
Made from a normal negative on normal printing paper, this print shows a full range of tones.

▲ **First interneg**
The same negative, contact printed on to 35mm lith film to produce a harsh, positive image on film.

▲ **Second interneg**
The positive image, contact printed on to another piece of lith film to make an even harsher negative.

▲ **Final result**
Print made on hard-grade printing paper, using the second interneg (*left*).

Solarization

SOLARIZATION, OR MORE ACCURATELY the Sabattier effect, produces a picture that has an intriguing mix of positive and negative aspects. It is achieved by exposing film or paper to white light part-way through development. This results in a darkening of the undeveloped areas of the image and a reversal of some of the tones. Also, a strong line appears between the borders of what should have been the light and dark areas.

The simplest (although a rather hit-and-miss) way of producing a solarized image is to expose a print in the normal way, and then briefly flash a white light over the developing dish halfway through development. You then continue development for the prescribed time, before washing and fixing the print in the normal way.

A better technique is to first expose a sheet of lith film under the enlarger (see p. 133). Develop this normally for half the correct development time, and then expose the sheet of film, while still in the developer tray, to white light from the enlarger for the same period as the original exposure. Then continue development and the other processing steps normally. A test strip can be made at the start to determine the best exposure on to the lith film.

The solarized negative can then either be contact printed with photographic paper, or contact printed with another sheet of lith film to make an intermediate negative (interneg) that shows the original tones reversed. If you are making a print from this interneg, a hard grade of paper usually produces the best results.

DIGITAL NOTES

• Solarization can be recreated in the digital darkroom. The easiest way to do this is to use the Curves adjustment found on top-end manipulation packages.

• To produce the half-negative, half-positive effect you create a U-shaped graph in the Curves window using a number of different anchor points to distort the traditional diagonal line.

• Individual anchor points can then be moved up and down to create even weirder effects.

◄ **Solarized result**
In this solarized print you can see that some of the image has remained normal in appearance while other parts have been partially reversed. Note how the technique introduces a sharp line, known as a Mackie line, between light and dark tones in some places.

Posterization

POSTERIZATION TAKES LITH FILM techniques a step further. With posterization, the image still shows a stark black and white effect, but this is combined with just a few well-defined intermediate shades of grey.

To prevent the process becoming too complicated, it is best to make a posterized print showing just three tones. Begin by exposing a conventional negative on to three sheets of lith film (*see p. 133*). One film should be overexposed, one normally exposed and one underexposed. By doing this, one of the films will favour only the shadows,

another the mid-tones and shadows, and the final film will favour only the highlights.

After processing, you will have 'density separations' of the original image. Posterization depends on printing each film in turn in exact register with the others. Holes are sometimes punched at the edge of the film to help assure perfect alignment with each print using a 'pin register'. When contact printing each sheet on to the paper, determine an exposure for each that will produce only a mid-grey image, to prevent the final print being too dark.

◄ Separation 1
The first lith negative was exposed to record the pale tones only.

◄ Separation 2
The second lith negative was exposed to record the mid-tones and shadows only.

◄ Separation 3
The third lith negative was exposed to record the dark tones only.

▲ Final result
This image was made by printing the three separations (*left*) on to a piece of normal-contrast paper. Each separation was exposed to produce a mid-grey tone only.

Spotting and retouching

EVEN THE MOST METICULOUS printer can end up with images that need retouching. Specks of dust adhering to the negatives as they dry will appear on the print as white dots; scratches on the negative emulsion might appear as fine black lines. It pays to these by cleaning negatives, negative carriers and lenses scrupulously, and handling negatives with reverent care. But with a little practice you can can disguise most of these almost inevitable blemishes.

For prints on matt, fibre-based paper, you can use a soft lead pencil to retouch white marks. Different grades of pencil can create a number of shades of grey – a 6B pencil looking darker than a 2B, for example.

For glossy prints, or those made on resin-coated paper, you need a tube of black watercolour

◄ Using a brush
Use a fine brush to gradually build up the area to be retouched by making a series of minute dots. Do not try to paint out the fault with larger brush strokes, since the result will be crude and obvious.

► Using a scalpel
For black specks, use a scalpel to gently scrape away the surface of the paper's emulsion before building up the tone again.

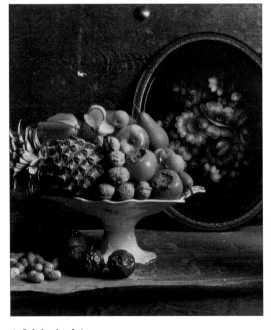

▲ Original print
Just as it came from the processing tray – a print in need of retouching to remove the prominent dust speck on the background wood.

▲ After retouching
This is the same print after retouching with a fine brush and watercolour paints. The dust speck is now completely invisible.

SPOTTING AND RETOUCHING

paint or special retouching paint (available from specialist photographic dealers).

Always use the finest brush available (a size 0 or 1 is ideal) and build up the area to be retouched with a series of minute dots, overlapping them for a darker tone. Practise on a piece of scrap paper to ensure that paint is mixed to the right consistency.

For black marks, use white paint. Alternatively, use a sharp scalpel to scratch the surface of the print gently; this is a technique that works better on fibre-based rather than resin-coated paper.

These days, only the most basic retouching is ever done on the print or the negative. It is so easy to remove blemishes using digital cloning techniques (see pages 148–9) that badly damaged prints and negatives are digitized and then restored using manipulation software.

▲ **Cracked with age**
This early 20th-century photograph, for which no negative now exists, has been damaged by years of neglect. It makes a prime candidate for computerized retouching.

◀ **After restoration**
The same picture as above, after being digitally scanned on to the computer and retouched with a manipulation program, probably looks better now than it did when originally taken.

Toning

PERHAPS THE BEST-KNOWN toner is sepia. This is the substance that produces the brown images we associate with early photographic processes. But sepia is not the only toner – black and white prints can be coloured red, blue, or green . . . and many more colours besides.

Toning works quite simply by converting the silver that makes up the black, and all the intermediate tones of an image to a chemical dye of a specific colour. There are several methods of toning a black and white print, but the most common are the single-solution and the two-bath methods.

Toning is not simply a way of adding a colour wash to a print. Many of the processes – such as selenium and gold toners – are primarily used as a way of extending the life expectancy of a print. Other toners are used to change the tonal balance of the image.

All toning processes can be carried out in daylight. And although the procedure is easy to follow, consistent results are often hard to achieve.

▲ **The original image**
This is the original black and white print before beginning a sepia-toning process – a two-bath method.

▲ **After bleaching**
The original image has been bleached to convert the black silver to silver bromide, which can then be toned.

◀ **After toning**
After immersion in the sepia toner, all the silver-based areas of the image have been rendered in various shades of brown. The coloration is now very much in keeping with the actual content of the photograph, which a decidedly old-fashioned feel to it.

DIGITAL NOTES

• To tone a digital black and white image, the image is first converted from a grayscale file to a colour (RGB) one. This is a simple, one-step procedure. Colour can then be added by tweaking the red, green and blue channels by different amounts, using the Curves or Levels adjustments.

• Some programs can create duotones and tritones from grayscale images (see p. 152).

▲ Blue toner
This striking image is the result of using an iron metal toner solution. The length of time the print remains in the toner is one of the factors that determines the strength of colour achieved.

▶ Red toner
Red toning has transformed this black and white print. This type of effect is possible using a nickel toner solution – another type of metal toner.

▲ Silver paper base
A similar effect can be achieved by using specialized printing papers with coloured bases. This print was made on a sheet of paper with a silver base.

▲ Gold paper base
This image was printed on gold based paper. Whereas toning affects the blacks and greys, this technique retains the tones and alters the paper's base colour.

Hand colouring

I N AN AGE when colour prints are the norm, it seems perverse to hand colour black and white images. However, hand colouring – once the only way to produce colour photographs – has today become an art form.

It is, of course, possible to colour an entire photograph, but a more creative effect can often be achieved by leaving most of the print in its original form and merely colouring selective areas – the eyes or lips in a portrait, for example.

Because of its plastic base, resin-coated paper is not suitable. Watercolours can be used on a damp print, while oil colours work best on dry prints. Even felt-tip pens can be used for hand-colouring purposes.

▲ The original image
This image makes an ideal subject for hand colouring.

▲ Soak the paper
Before using water-based paint, soak the print and then work on the image while it is still damp.

▲ Build up the effect
Work on small areas of the print at a time and think about colouring only small sections.

▶ The final result
This partially hand-coloured result has real impact.

Dry mounting

FOR THOSE CONTEMPLATING entering their pictures in exhibitions, or perhaps displaying them on a wall, mounting the print is essential. There are several ways of doing this. You can spray an even coat of a dry-mounting medium on the back of the print, and then press it down on to a piece of stiff card. A better method, however, is to use heat-sensitive dry-mounting tissue. Many top galleries and photographers find this old-fashioned method the best way of keeping the print flat.

Dry-mounting tissue comes in sheets and has a coating of shellac on either side covered by a thin layer of wax. The tissue is placed between the print and the mount and, when heat is applied, the wax melts, releasing the gum and bonding the print and mount. The print can be flush-mounted so that it covers all the mount, or it can be positioned centrally on the mount, leaving a border all around.

A dry-mounting press can be used. This not only applies the necessary heat, it also exerts an even pressure over the entire surface to be bonded, thus keeping the print completely flat against its mount. For those on a budget, a domestic iron, set to a low heat, can be used for the purpose.

1 Place the tissue on the back of the print. Use a tacking iron to attach it to the corners of the print.

2 With the print face-up on the mount, lift each corner and tack the tissue to the mount.

3 Place tracing paper over the print and apply heat to the whole surface at the iron's lowest setting.

4 Use a metal ruler and a sharp blade to trim the print and mount together for a flush effect.

▶ **Ready for the show**
Here is the final print, mounted and ready to be exhibited or hung on the wall at home.

The digital darkroom

THE DIGITAL EQUIVALENT of the darkroom is a computer running an image manipulation program. Just as under the enlarger, the on-screen tools allow you to crop the image. You can shade (or dodge) and burn-in areas of the image, and print different sections at different contrast levels – and you can tone the final picture in all manner of hues.

Despite the similarities, however, the digital darkroom allows far more control over how your raw image is produced than was ever possible with a negative under an enlarger. It can correct errors in exposure, magic away mistakes in composition, and turn weak images into powerful ones. But as well as making up for the mortal failings of the person behind the camera, digital manipulation has brought a new level of artistry to photography.

Unlike a real darkroom, you don't need much in the way of special facilities to set up a digital workstation. Any relatively recent home computer is more than up to the task – although the more processing power and memory it has, the faster the program will work when handling large files. A standard colour screen will suffice – but it is essential that this is set up with a neutral desktop colour and away from strong window reflections; it should also be calibrated so that colours are displayed accurately. All editing tools can be controlled using a normal keyboard and mouse – although some photographers prefer a graphics tablet for more precise control over what they are doing on screen.

▶ **Digital manipulation**
Digital manipulation software allows you to control contrast within the image. Here a stark, high-contrast silhouette has been created against a background with a more balanced distribution of greys.

Digital darkroom tools

IT IS NOT NECESSARY TO USE a digital camera to enter the world of computer manipulation. Negatives and slides (whether on colour or black and white film) can be turned into digital files using a scanning process. This can be done by your processing laboratory – it is cheaper to have it done at the time your films are processed, but it may be more cost-effective simply to get the images that you actually want to work on scanned. Alternatively, you can buy scanners for use at home (see box).

▶ **Graphics tablet**
Optional alternative to the mouse for controlling manipulation tools.

SCANNING

• Desktop flatbed scanners are primarily designed for digitizing prints and other artwork. Some have transparency hoods for scanning negatives and slides – but resolution may be low.

• A film scanner is specifically designed for scanning slides or negatives at high resolution.

• Scanning at the maximum available resolution gives you more scope for cropping the picture, and will allow you to print out bigger blow-ups without a visible deterioration in image quality.

• Lower resolutions can be used when preparing an image for emailing or for on-screen use. But it is often better to manipulate at a high resolution - then re-save at a lower resolution later. This gives more options as to how the image can be used in the future.

• The best film scanners can automatically detect and correct for dust and scratches – however, this facility does not work with many black and white films (so should be switched off).

◀ **Scanning box**
Film scanners can produce high-resolution digital files from negatives and slides; colour material can be scanned and converted to black and white once in a digital form. Different models can handle different formats. This box can handle both 35mm and APS film.

DIGITAL DARKROOM TOOLS

◄ Which computer?
Some photographers prefer Macs, others stick with PCs. The best-known software programs, such as Photoshop and Photoshop Elements, are equally at home on either platform. Here Photoshop is being used to tone a grayscale image on a Mac (*see pp152–3*).

PRINTING

• Most desktop colour inkjet printers are capable of producing reasonable prints.

• Special photo-quality inkjet printers are able to give a higher resolution, which is good for producing larger prints, and to provide borderless images.

• Whichever inkjet printer you use, the type of paper used is key. As a rough rule, the more you pay, the brighter and glossier your results will be, the longer the print will last, and the thicker the paper will be.

• It is essential that you tell the printer software which type of paper you have loaded. However, you must calibrate the printer software colour settings if you want to ensure that the printed result matches the on-screen image as closely as possible.

• For the most consistent and trouble-free results, it pays to use the printer manufacturer's own ink cartridges rather than cheaper 'compatible' products.

• You do not have to print your manipulated images yourself. High street laboratories can work from a copy of the image saved back to your digital camera's memory card – or from a recorded CD or DVD. Online labs let you upload your images over the web, and the prints are then posted back to you.

◄ Printers
Special photographic printers are not expensive, but ink and paper can prove costly. Inks specifically designed for black and white printing are available, although normal colour and black inks will do.

Colour conversions

FILM PHOTOGRAPHERS have always been able to produce black and white prints from colour film. The process, however, is a laborious one – with the first step being to create an interneg, by photographing the slide or print with black and white film. In the digital darkroom, however, colour images can be converted from colour to 'grayscale' in a one-step, near-instantaneous operation.

The ease of the conversion process means that many photographers shoot colour images with their digital cameras, rather than switch to black and white mode – even if the shot is going to be printed in monochrome

This way of working provides the advantage that the colour information can be used to enhance the conversion process. Digital images, whether produced by scanner or camera, are effectively three pictures in one – one in red, one in green, and one in blue. These three combine to produce a full-colour 'RGB' image. Each of the colour 'channels' is effectively a monochrome image – capable of producing a black and white conversion that is slightly different from that produced by either of the other two channels. One channel may also be less grainy than the others. Most

significantly, each colour in the image is produced in a different shade of grey in each of the channels.

By mixing the three different channels in different proportions, you can therefore change how dark or light different areas of the image appear in the black and white conversion. The effect is similar to that obtained by using colour filters in front of the camera when using black-and-white film (see pp 38–9).

Not all image manipulation programs, however, are capable of accessing and adjusting the colour channel information directly. This facility is normally only found on more expensive software packages aimed at the professional user (such as Adobe Photoshop). However, a similar result can be used with the Hue/Saturation/Brightness (or HSB) control provided on most budget editing programs (such as Adobe Photoshop Elements). This control effectively gives you six channels – blue, cyan, green, yellow, red, magenta – plus a master to manipulate all of them simultaneously. With this, you use the Master's saturation control to turn the image to monochrome. Then the brightness of each of the six colours is reduced or increased to brighten or darken different areas of tone within the image.

▲ Grayscale conversion
Programs provide a one-step conversion to mono; this discards the colour information, so take care to back up the original.

▲ ▼ Colour channels

The full-colour RGB image (above) consists of three
monochrome channels (below), one for the reds, one for
the greens, and the other for the blues.

WHICH SOFTWARE?

Some image editing programs can cost more
than your computer. Furthermore, you will
discover that there are hundreds of utilities
available to add extra functionality to the best-
known programs, automating complex
corrections, or generating useful special effects.

However, it is not essential to spend a fortune
on software. Often scanners, digital cameras and
photo-quality printers come bundled with
powerful packages that provide all that you really
need to start work in the digital darkroom.

You will also find that most software titles can
be downloaded on a trial basis from the author's
or distributor's internet site – allowing you to
assess the suitability and value of a program
before you buy it. Even the best-selling Adobe
Photoshop and Photoshop Elements titles can be
test driven in this way.

▲ ▼ Channel mixing in Photoshop Elements

Create a monochrome image by turning the Master
saturation level right down (below). Then change
brightness of different areas of tone using the
Lightness controls of particular colours (bottom).

Digital retouching

EDITING PROGRAMS are capable of altering your images in all manner of ways, but although psychedelic special effects and artistic photomontages catch the eye, it is the minor corrections possible in the digital darkroom that prove the most useful.

The advantage of a digital image is that it is made up of millions of squares of colour (or pixels) – each of which can be changed to a different tone if need be. It is this amount of precise control that makes computer techniques so different from those used in a traditional darkroom. Retouching, in particular, is such a straightforward process in the digital domain that the composition of most images can be improved in ways that wouldn't be attempted with old-fashioned spotting techniques (*see pp 136–7*).

Once you get used to the process, it will even make you change the way you shoot. There is no need, for instance, to compromise on viewpoint just to eliminate an unwanted crane from a city skyscape – when you know that the offending piece of machinery can be removed digitally. The process will also allow you to revitalize damaged negatives and remove annoying details from shots that previously wouldn't have been considered worth printing.

▲ ▼ Removing dust and scratches
Photoshop's Healing Brush and Clone tools were used to meticulously clean up the sky in this scanned black and white negative.

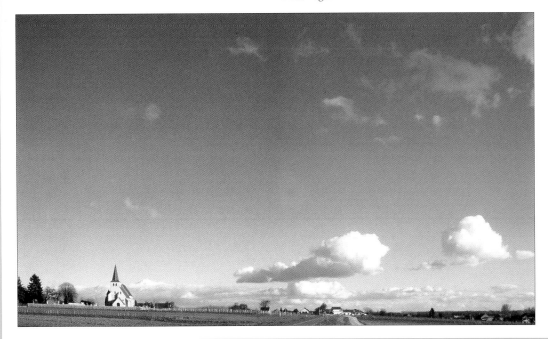

DIGITAL RETOUCHING

Rather than working on individual pixels, the key technique in digital retouching is to use the editing software's Clone tool. This allows you to cover offending areas of the image, replacing them with other pixels from the same picture. The idea is to imagine what would be in that part of picture if the blemish or eyesore were not there. Telephone wires can be painted away using nearby areas of sky as the source, for example. Graffiti can be replaced using clean bricks from the same wall.

The great advantage of working digitally is that it does not matter if you make a mistake. You can go back a step if the cloning doesn't look right by simply using the Undo command. With some programs you can go back multiple steps using the History window. Corrections can be isolated in a layer, so that these can be edited or abandoned without affecting anything else you have done to the image. And by working on a copy of the file, you can always go back to square one, as the original will remain as scanned or shot.

▲ ▼ Using the Clone stamp
You can remove most annoying intrusions from your composition. Here the wheelbarrow was taken out by cloning replacement material from the surrounding area; the fisherman was then made to disappear.

BLURRING THE BACKGROUND

The sharpness of a background can be controlled at the time of shooting by altering your shooting distance, the aperture and the focal length of the lens. However, there are times when elements in the distance end up being less out of focus than you would like. The Gaussian Blur filter, found in many editing packages, allows you to de-focus areas in a photograph so that they don't detract from the main subject. A blurred version of the whole image is created on a separate layer, and a copy of the sharp version is placed on top of this. Distracting areas of the sharp copy are then removed using the Eraser tool. This works as a paintbrush, and can be set to remove the sharp version entirely, or set at partial opacity to create different levels of blur (allowing you to recreate the effects of depth of field more authentically).

▲ ▼ Selective focus
The background in the shot above was isolated using the Lasso tool. This selected area was then made less sharp using the Gaussian Blur filter. This has created a stronger portrait as the backdrop is less intrusive.

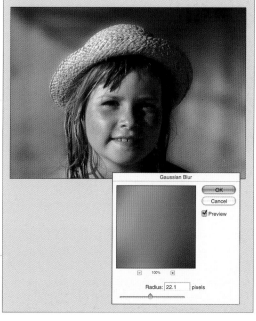

Tonal adjustments

DIGITAL MANIPULATION SOFTWARE frequently provides a multitude of different ways of achieving similar effects. This is especially true when it comes to making exposure and contrast adjustments, where a wide range of tools is provided for changing the tonal range of the image. The route you take is a matter of taste and confidence, but some methods provide more sophisticated control than others.

A well-exposed image should ideally include small areas of bright white and jet black, with the majority of tones spread relatively evenly in between. The Levels control shows you graphically whether this has actually been achieved, and provides a straightforward way of improving things if not. Digital images provide 256 levels of grey for each pixel – with 255 being pure white and 0 representing the deepest black. A histogram shows how many pixels you have of each density in the image (a similar readout is provided with digital SLRs as a way of assessing exposure). If the graph does not stretch from one extreme to another, you can move the white pointer and black pointer inwards to compensate; the effect that this will have is previewed in the on-screen image.

In black and white photography, you will frequently want to alter the exposure and contrast of certain areas differently to others. In the traditional darkroom this is achieved by shading (dodging) and burning-in, and by selectively changing the filtration used with the variable contrast paper. In the digital darkroom, each exposure change can be made on a separate adjustment layer – allowing you to mask or partially mask areas where this adjustment has less or no effect, with ultimate precision. You can therefore use different Levels adjustments in a single picture.

A more sophisticated control still is the Curves adjustment found on professional image editing software. This combines the functionality of Levels adjustment with the ability to lighten and darken a range of mid-tones without affecting the white and black in the image.

▲ Dull print
A muddy image may look reasonable in isolation, but the histogram shows the truth. All the tones are bunched in the middle, with no dark greys, blacks, or lighter tones.

▲ After Levels adjustment
By moving the black and white pointers under the histogram inwards, the image is improved. The wider range of tones is preferable to what we had before.

◄ Original shot
As is often the case with black and white landscapes, the sky needs special treatment. Otherwise, as in this example, it appears so light in the image that cloud detail is lost.

◄▲ After adjustment
Adjusting the Levels at the top of the picture creates a sky with more punch. A mask is created so that only the selected part of the image is affected (above), then the black and white histogram points are pulled in to increase contrast (top).

◄▲ Using Curves
Adjusting Curves allows a more detailed correction of tone than is possible with Levels. By altering the straight line that is presented to you before any manipulation is made, you can effectively darken and lighten different tones independently. The S-curve applied to this shot of a flower is a standard adjustment for the black and white photographer. It increases the darkness of the dark greys and lightens the light greys – without affecting the pure whites and blacks in the image.

Special effects

DIGITAL EDITING SOFTWARE allows the photographer to recreate a wide range of traditional darkroom effects at a click of a button – as well as providing new ways to manipulate an image.

Toning, for example, is done easily on the computer – without toxic chemicals and unpredictable results. The simplest way to produce a toned monochrome image from a colour picture is to use the Hue/Saturation control. This provides a Colorize option, which when selected allows you to choose the colour and intensity of the toned conversion.

A more sophisticated option is available with professional editing packages. This allows you to create duotone or tritone effects from a grayscale image. You choose the two or three colours you wish to work with – with the ways these appear in the image being manipulated using Curve controls (*see p 151*). It is important to realize, however, that unlike metal toners, digital equivalents do not affect the longevity or tonal range of the picture.

Many of the more breathtaking effects created by editing programs are made possible by 'filters'. A range of these is supplied with most packages - with others available to buy or download separately. Some recreate camera effects – such as zoom bursts and panning. Others mimic darkroom techniques such as solarization and bas relief. Others create new effects – such as making your image resemble a stained-glass window, a watercolour painting, or a charcoal drawing. Not all, however, work effectively with monochrome images.

The filter that is used most by photographers is undoubtedly the Unsharp Mask (or USM) control. Despite its name, this facility is used as a way of sharpening a digital image. It is not, however, designed for rescuing out-of-focus pictures. All digital images are inherently soft – and although scanners and cameras usually provide an option for sharpening them electronically at the time of acquisition, it is best to leave this job to the USM filter. The fact is that some images will need more sharpening that others; you will need to sharpen more if the picture is to be printed than if it is simply going to be viewed on screen, for instance. The effect is best applied as the last step after all other manipulation has been completed. However, USM can provide effects of its own. Over-sharpening the image can be one of the most effective ways to add grain to an image, in order to provide atmosphere and texture.

◀ **Toning using Hue/Saturation**
Photoshop Elements allows you to create toned images from colour originals with the minimimum of fuss. Check the Colorize option in the Hue/Saturation dialogue box, and you get a sepia image. The colour of the toner can then be adjusted using the Hue slider, and the strength of colour is tweaked using the Saturation control.

◀ Toning using Duotone control

Photoshop allows you to create toned images from grayscale originals. Two or more coloured 'inks' are combined to create the image. A different Curve adjustment (*see page 151*) is applied to each colour, giving a subtle range of colouration in the mid-tones.

▼ Over-sharpening for effect

The Unsharp Mask is normally applied subtly to improve sharpness prior to printing or online display. Typical settings are an Amount of 50–150%, a Radius of 0.5–4, and a Threshold of between 0–2.

▲ Artistic filter effects

Photoshop and Photoshop Elements provide a number of artistic filters that make your photographs appear like paintings or drawings. Further effects can be added by using compatible 'plug-ins' produced by other software developers to work with these programs. This effect was created using Adobe's own Dry Brush filter.

Glossary

Angle of view The amount of a scene that can be encompassed by a particular lens focal length. A wide-angle lens has a greater angle of view than a telephoto.

Aperture A gap of variable diameter formed by a series of overlapping metal leaves within a lens. The size of the aperture determines the intensity of light reaching the film or digital image sensor.

Burning-in Increasing the amount of exposure received by a part of a print in order to darken that area of the image.

CCD (charge coupled device) Light sensitive chip commonly used in digital cameras.

CMOS (complementary metal oxide semiconductor) Light-sensitive chip commonly used in digital cameras.

Chromogenic Photographic film that forms a negative from coloured dyes during processing.

Contact sheet A sheet of images the same size as the negatives, produced by placing the negatives in contact with printing paper and exposing them to light. Used to select images for enlargement.

Contrast The difference in brightness between the brightest highlights and deepest shadows in a subject, negative or print.

Cropping Selectively enlarging an image so that unwanted parts of the subject are not recorded on the printing paper, or are cut from a digital image

Depth of field The zone of acceptably sharp focus that extends both in front of and behind the point of actual focus. Depth of field is variable, increasing as focal lengths become shorter, apertures smaller and focal distance farther from the camera.

Developer A chemical solution used to convert the latent image on exposed film or photographic paper into a visible image.

Development The chemical treatment and mechanical procedure that converts a latent photographic image into a visible image.

Emulsion The light-sensitive coating on film and photographic paper consisting of silver halide grains suspended in gelatine.

Exposure The total amount of light reaching the film or photographic paper. This is determined by the size of aperture and the length of time it is left open.

File format The 'language' in which a digital image file is saved. The format affects which programs can open the file, and the size and detail in the image. Common types include RAW, Tiff and JPEG.

Fixer A chemical solution used in film and print processing. The action of the fixer converts unexposed and undeveloped silver halides into water-soluble salts that can be rinsed away, thus making the image stable.

f numbers A series of numbers found on the aperture control ring of a lens. Turning the ring to the next higher number (from f5.6 to f8, for example)

halves the area of the aperture and so halves the intensity of light reaching the film (or paper with an enlarger lens). Also known as f stops, which gives rise to the expression 'stopping down' – making the aperture smaller by selecting a higher f number setting.

Fogging Subjecting film or photographic paper to non-image-forming light. This creates an area of uniform density. The same effect can be caused by exposing the film or paper to certain chemicals or chemical fumes.

Grain The visual appearance of the individual clumps of silver halide crystals making up the photographic emulsion. Also refers to visible 'noise' in a digital image.

Hand colouring Applying colour – watercolour, oil, acrylic and so on – to a black and white image.

High key An image in which the tones are predominantly light. The effects of a high-key image can be enhanced by slight overexposure.

ISO An abbreviation for International Standards Organization. An internationally agreed system of rating the speed, or sensitivity to light, of film. A doubling of ISO number (from 200 to 400, for example) indicates a doubling of film speed. Also used as a measure of the sensitivity or speed of a digital camera's imaging chip.§

JPEG (Joint Photographic Experts Group) A file format commonly used by digital cameras. Variable amounts of compression are used to reduce the size of the file.

GLOSSARY

LCD (liquid crystal display) Panel giving information about camera functions. Colour LCDs are used to preview and replay images taken on digital cameras.

Lith film An extremly high-contrast film, which, when used in conjunction with a special lith developer, produces images that consist of either black or white, with no intermediate shades of grey.

Low key An image in which the tones are predominantly dark. The effects of a low-key image can be enhanced by slight underexposure.

Megabyte Measurement of digital memory; same as 1,048,576 bytes.

Megapixel Units used to measure the maximum resolution of a digital camera's CCD or CMOS image sensor; a million pixels.

Multiple printing A print composed of images from more than one negative. Masks are used to shield parts of the printing paper that have already been exposed each time a new negative is projected down from the enlarger.

Negative A film image in which the subject tones or colours are reversed. A black and white negative will have dense areas of tone corresponding to bright subject highlights, and areas of clear film corresponding to dense subject shadows.

Overexposure Allowing the film or photographic paper to receive too much light, giving rise to a pale-toned result.

Paper grade Describes the contrast-recording ability of photographic paper. Grades 0–1 are soft; 2–3 are normal; 4 and above are hard.

Pixel A single light-sensitive element in a digital camera's sensor. The basic unit used in measuring the resolution from a digital camera or in a digital image.

Posterization A print that contains areas of clearly demarcated flat tones, as opposed to natural-looking continuous tones.

Print A positive image on paper, producing by shining light through a negative.

RAW High-quality file format available on digital SLRs.

Retouching Using dyes or pigments, usually with a fine brush, to remove blemishes from a negative or print.

Sabattier effect A darkroom technique in which a part-developed image is re-exposed to white light to produce a part-negative, part-positive result.

Safelight A low-wattage darkroom light filtered so that its colour will not affect the photographic emulsions being used. Although light output is usually very low, it is sufficient to allow the darkroom to be used conveniently.

Sandwich printing Combining two or more film images in the enlarger and printing them simultaneously on to one piece of photographic paper.

Shading (dodging) Decreasing the amount of exposure received by a part of the print in order to lighten that part of the image. Also known as shading.

Shutter speed The length of time the camera's shutter stays open, allowing light from the lens aperture

to affect the film. The shutter speed dial is calibrated in speeds of fractions of a second, or multiples of complete seconds. Changing the dial to the next setting either doubles or halves the length of time the shutter remains open.

Solarization Causing the tones of a photographic image to reverse through massive overexposure. This term is often incorrectly applied to the Sabattier effect.

Speed Refers to the light sensitivity of film or to the widest maximum aperture a particular lens has to offer.

Spotting An after-treatment for negatives or prints in which small dark or light marks are removed using dyes, pigments, inks or pencils.

Stop bath A chemical solution used to halt the action of film or paper developer when the right image density has been reached.

Test strip A strip of printing paper with a range of exposures, used as an exposure guide for making an enlargement.

TIFF (tagged image file format) High-quality, but memory-hungry, file format that can be used on some digital cameras.

Tonal range The shades of grey between black and white contained in a negative or print.

Toning Using chemicals to change the colour of a black and white image.

Underexposure Allowing the film or photographic paper to receive too little light, giving rise to a dark-toned result.

Index

INDEX

INDEX

INDEX

Acknowledgements

The author would like to thank Roger Bristow, Phil Kay and Rod Teasdale for styling and designing the book; Chris George for editorial work and assistance on the text; and Jenny MacIntosh for her work as photographic assistant.

Studio photography and darkroom facilities were provided by Simon Logan and Harry Mears of Saffron Photography Ltd, with assistance from Simon Nicol. The illustrations of negative faults were produced by Peter Elgar, the posterized and multiple prints by Harbutt and Grier, and the diagrams of darkroom set-ups by Craige Quainton. Special thanks are due to KJP for their very generous loan of darkroom equipment.